Travel Guide

SCOTLAND

Robin Gauldie

First edition published in 2001
by New Holland Publishers (UK) Ltd
London • Cape Town • Sydney • Auckland

10 9 8 7 6 5 4 3 2 1

Garfield House, 86 Edgeware Road
London W2 2EA
United Kingdom

80 McKenzie Street
Cape Town 8001
South Africa

14 Aquatic Drive
Frenchs Forest, NSW 2086
Australia

218 Lake Road
Northcote, Auckland
New Zealand

Distributed in the USA by
The Globe Pequot Press
Connecticut

Copyright © 2001 in text: Robin Gauldie
Copyright © 2001 in maps:
Globetrotter Travel Maps
Copyright © 2001 in photographs:
Individual photographers as credited (right).
Copyright © 2001 New Holland Publishers (UK) Ltd

ISBN 1 85974 656 X

Cover: *The ruins of Kilchurn Castle, Loch Awe.*
Title Page: *A kilted piper in typical Highland dress.*

Commissioning Editor: Tim Jollands
Manager Globetrotter Maps: John Loubser
Managing Editor: Thea Grobbelaar
Editors: Mary Duncan, Sara Harper
Picture Researcher: Sonya Meyer
Design and DTP: Benjamin Latham
Cartographer: Carl Germishuys
Proofreader: Thea Grobbelaar

Reproduction by Hirt & Carter (Pty) Ltd, Cape Town
Printed and bound in Hong Kong by Sing Cheong
Printing Co. Ltd.

Photographic Credits:
Sylvia Cordaiy PL/James de Bounevialle: page 8;
Sylvia Cordaiy PL/Humphrey Evans: page 59; **Sylvia
Cordaiy PL/John Farmar:** page 49; **Sylvia Cordaiy PL/
Les Gibbon:** page 48; **Sylvia Cordaiy PL/C J Hall:**
page 15; **Sylvia Cordaiy PL/Roger Halls:** page 120;
Sylvia Cordaiy PL/J Howard: pages 52, 72; **Sylvia
Cordaiy PL/P S Linfoot:** page 84; **Sylvia Cordaiy PL/
James Murdoch:** pages 6, 23, 25, 27, 33, 53; **Sylvia
Cordaiy PL/Edward O'Neill:** page 44; **Sylvia Cordaiy
PL/Howard O'Neill:** page 60; **Sylvia Cordaiy PL/John
Parker:** page 46; **Sylvia Cordaiy PL/David Saunders:**
page 9; **Sylvia Cordaiy PL/Geoffrey Taunton:** pages 39,
61; **Sylvia Cordaiy PL/Helga Willcocks:** page 24;
Sylvia Cordaiy PL/Julian Worker: page 50; **Gallo/
Tony Stone Images/Joe Cornish:** title page; **Gallo/
Tony Stone Images/John Lawrence:** cover; **Photo
Access/Michael Hart:** page 111; **PhotoBank/Adrian
Baker:** pages 13, 19, 54 (top), 70, 71, 74, 78, 83, 85, 88,
95, 98, 100, 103, 116; **PhotoBank/Jeanetta Baker:** pages
69, 89, 92; **PhotoBank/Peter Baker:** pages 11, 20, 21, 30,
34, 35, 36, 40, 41, 51, 56, 58, 64, 68, 73, 81, 87, 96, 97, 99,
101, 104, 105, 108, 114, 115, 117, 119 (bottom); **Wouter
van Warmelo:** pages 4, 10, 12, 14, 16, 17, 18, 22, 28, 37,
38, 42, 43, 75, 112, 113 (top and bottom), 119 (top);
Andrew Wheeler: pages 26, 54 (bottom), 66 (top and
bottom); **Lawson Wood:** pages 29, 102.

CONTENTS

1. Introducing Scotland 5
The Land 6
History in Brief 10
Government and Economy 18
The People 20

2. Edinburgh 31
The Royal Mile 32
The Grassmarket and
the University Area 37
Calton Hill 39
Princes Street 40
The New Town 41
Cramond 43
Linlithgow 44

3. The Border Country 47
North Berwick and Kelso 48
Jedburgh 49
Melrose and Galashiels 49
Selkirk and Peebles 50
Dumfries and Galloway 51
Ayrshire 53

4. Glasgow 57
Central Glasgow 58
West of the Centre 59
South of the Clyde 62

5. Central Scotland 65
Argyll 66
Loch Lomond and the Trossachs 68
Stirling and Around 70
Dunfermline and Around 71
The Neuk of Fife 73
St Andrews 75

6. Tayside and Grampian 79
Perth and Perthshire 80
Dundee and Angus 82
Deeside and the Northeast 86
Aberdeen and Around 88

7. The Highlands 93
Fort William and Lochaber 94
Fort Augustus and Loch Ness 96
Inverness and Around 97
The Badenoch Hoghlands 98
The West Coast 99
Ullapool and Around 101
Caithness and the East Coast 102

**8. Western and
Northern Isles 109**
Islay and Jura 110
Mull 112
Skye 113
The Outer Hebrides 115
Orkney 117
Shetland 119

Travel Tips 122

Index 127

1
Introducing Scotland

Scotland is one of the world's most romantic, and romanticized countries, with a reputation that far overshadows its size. For a **small nation** located on the outer fringes of Europe, Scotland and its people have had an enormous impact on the world, whether as soldiers, scholars, writers and poets, inventors, economists or politicians.

This is a country with a fascinating and complex history of Scots and Picts, Vikings and Normans, proud resistance and bloody conquest, and above all of the survival of a **national culture** that refuses to give in. It is a land of great variety, from big, bustling cities bursting with vitality to tiny fishing villages tucked away in sheltered bays. In its hinterland are some of Europe's last empty spaces – **pocket wilderness** areas where red deer roam and golden eagles soar.

There are great stretches of empty Atlantic coastline and dramatic North Sea cliffs and crags teeming with seabirds and crowned with the ruins of **ancient castles**. And there are **dozens of islands**, some green and warmed by the tail end of the Gulf Stream, others mere rocky dots swept by the high seas. And there are its people – Scots all, but proud of a dozen or more regional identities, from the **Gaelic-speaking islanders** of Lewis to the **streetwise urbanites** of Glasgow.

Scotland at the beginning of the 21st century is a country rediscovering itself, with a new confidence in its identity, its culture, and its future. More than ever, it is a country waiting to be discovered.

TOP ATTRACTIONS

*** Edinburgh Castle: the best-known landmark of Scotland's capital.
*** Eilean Donan Castle: romantic ruin familiar from films and posters.
*** Burrell Collection, Glasgow: gorgeously eclectic array of art and artefacts.
*** The Cuillins, Skye: harshly beautiful hills.
*** Ben Nevis: Scotland's highest mountain.
** RRS Discovery, Dundee: the wooden ship that took Scott to the Antarctic.

Opposite: *Dollar Castle, the 15th-century stronghold of the Clan Campbell, near Stirling.*

NATIONAL TOURIST ROUTES

Scotland has twelve National Tourist Routes, all clearly and frequently marked by distinctive **brown signs bearing a thistle symbol**. They have been specially selected to take you off the less interesting main roads onto quieter, scenic routes through beautiful countryside with many attractions, from castles and distilleries to golf courses and the birthplaces of famous Scots. Many of these routes are featured in this guide, and can be found in information boxes in the relevant regional chapter.

Below: *Rannoch Moor, one of Scotland's wilderness areas, is a wild expanse of moorland and mountain – a favourite place for walking, cycling, canoeing and fishing.*

THE LAND

Scotland's border with England is along a diagonal line between the Solway Firth on the west coast and a point just to the north of Berwick-upon-Tweed on the east coast. Gretna Green, at the southernmost point of the border, is some 500km (310 miles) from London and 603km (375 miles) from Scotland's northernmost point, near John O'Groats.

Lochs and Islands

Three deep estuaries, or firths, are the main features of Scotland's eastern, North Sea coast. In the west, the Firth of Clyde opens into the Atlantic, while the northwest coast is a ragged fringe of narrow sea lochs and the innumerable islands, large and small, of the Inner and Outer Hebrides. The Orkney archipelago lies close to the north coast, and the Shetland Islands, far out in the North Sea, can claim to be Britain's most remote community.

Highlands and Lowlands

Strathmore (the name, in Gaelic, means 'great valley'), running diagonally between the northeast Lowlands near Aberdeen and the River Forth near Stirling, conveniently divides Highland from Lowland Scotland. To the north of this line, the country rises dramatically to the impressive ramparts of the **Grampian Mountains**.

The Great Glen, a chain of deep lochs running diagonally from the southwest to the head of the Moray Firth in the east, separates the Grampians from the northern Highlands.

The Old Red Sandstone of which the Highlands are largely formed is the oldest exposed rock in the world, and the Scottish mountains have been worn down by millions of years of erosion and glaciation.

Climate

Scotland's climate is significantly **colder** and **wetter** on average than that of southern England, with subzero temperatures possible, especially on higher ground, from October until May. All Scotland's major cities are on the coast, and the warming effect of the

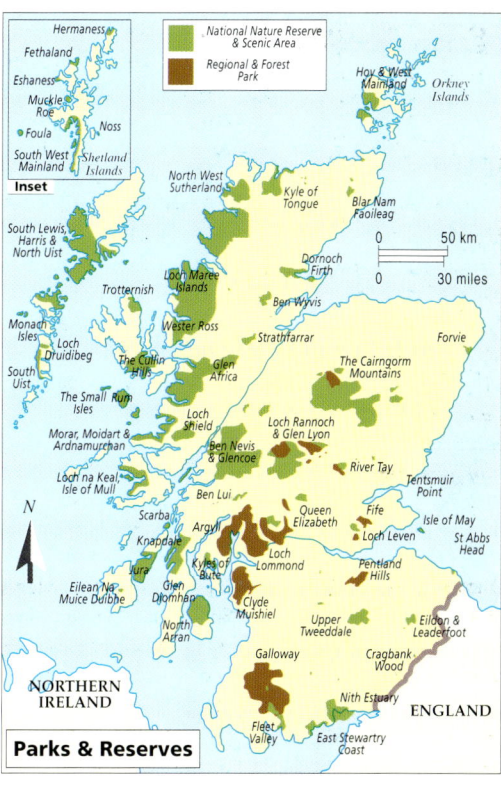

sea means that snow rarely affects Glasgow, Dundee or Edinburgh for long, although hills within sight of the city centre may be thickly covered.

Blizzards and extreme weather conditions are possible in hill country from at least October until late May and walkers planning even a short walk in the hills must be properly equipped. Days are noticeably shorter in the Scottish winter than in the south. **Rain** is possible at any time of year. The west coast, warmed by the last traces of the Gulf Stream, is notorious for its high rainfall. Overall, winter temperatures can occasionally drop as low as -10°C (-50°F) on high ground in winter, while summer temperatures rarely rise higher than 25°C (77°F).

PEAK PRACTICE

Scottish mountains can be very dangerous, and weather conditions can change rapidly. To avoid being stranded – or worse – on the mountains, never go climbing or hiking without warm, waterproof clothing, food, water and a whistle. Always tell someone where you are going and remember that even the most experienced climbers can run into difficulties.

Above: *Red deer roam in large numbers on the Highland hillsides.*

THE OLDEST TREE

Myth has it that Fortingall, about 20km (12 miles) west of Aberfeldy at the foot of Glen Lyon, is the birthplace of **Pontius Pilate**, whose father is supposed to have been a legionary officer stationed there. A huge yew tree in the churchyard of this attractive village with its thatched houses – most of them restored in 1900 – is claimed to be the oldest tree in Europe, more than 3000 years old. There is little evidence, however, to support either claim.

Flora and Fauna

As recently as 2000 years ago, much of the land was covered by beech, oak, ash, rowan, birch and pine. Today, only a fragment of this primeval mixed forest survives, its trees having been felled for fuel, timber or to clear grazing land. Large areas of rural Scotland are planted with uniform rows of conifers, but these monocultural woods are gradually giving way to more wildlife-friendly mixed woodland. The white bark of the **silver birch**, clinging to thin soil and almost bare rock where no other tree will grow, is characteristic of Highland woodland. And all those clichés about heather-covered hills are true – in summer, the hill country of Scotland really is ablaze with **purple heather**.

Scotland's low population pressure has allowed many bird and animal species that are now extinct in southern Britain to survive, while the country's unique mountain, moorland and marine habitats shelter species found nowhere else in Britain.

Red deer, conserved for shooting, roam in large numbers on Highland estates. Red and black grouse also owe their numbers to preservation as game birds, as do the huge numbers of pheasants seen on farmlands. Birds of prey include the **golden eagle**, found nowhere else in

Britain, and the osprey, successfully reintroduced during the 1960s. **White-headed sea eagles**, once extinct, have also been reintroduced from Scandinavia. Buzzards have also made a comeback and are seen in numbers throughout the eastern Lowlands. **Ptarmigan** and **capercaillie** are also seen on upland moors and pine forests. Seabirds include large gannet colonies on the Bass Rock in the Firth of Forth and on the west coast; puffin, guillemot and razorbill on sea cliffs; numerous gulls and terns and, in the north, the skua. Ducks and geese include pink-footed and greylag goose, numerous species of sea duck, and all three species of British swan.

In addition to mammal species found throughout Britain, Scotland is home to the **wild cat** and to Britain's largest **otter** population, found in fresh water and on the west coast. Marine mammals include grey and common seals, porpoises, common dolphins and, on the Moray Firth, one of only three groups of **bottlenose dolphins** in British waters. Killer whales or orcas are very occasionally seen, giving their name to the Orkney islands. Less fortunate species include Scotland's wolves, the last of which was shot as recently as 1743, and the Scottish beaver, extinct by the 17th century, and it has been suggested that the beaver, like the osprey, could be reintroduced from Scandinavian stock.

Domesticated breeds that are unique to Scotland include the shaggy, red-haired **Highland cattle** and the big-horned **Soay sheep** once farmed in the Western Isles. **Salmon** are found off the coasts of Scotland and spawn in Scottish rivers, and **brown trout**, found in rivers and lochs, are also eagerly sought by anglers.

SHETLAND SEABIRDS

Shetland is a nesting place for more than 200 seabird species, with a puffin population of more than 250,000 and gannet colonies of over 30,000 birds nesting on its black cliffs. Other species include numerous gulls, fulmars, storm petrels, shags, guillemots, kittiwakes, razorbills, cormorants, and terns, as well as ferocious great skuas (also called bonxies) which will attack humans near their nests. Red-throated divers, merlins, whimbrels, red-necked phalaropes and grey phalaropes breed inland.

Below: *Puffins roost on sea cliffs on Scotland's isles and on the east and west coasts of the mainland.*

Below: *This memorial near Fort William commemorates World War II commandoes who trained nearby.*

HISTORY IN BRIEF

Scotland's history seems designed to confuse, and the Scots themselves have trouble unravelling the thread of history from the tangled myths of Caledonia's misty past. Little is known of the earliest Stone Age and Bronze Age inhabitants of Scotland, and there is is no written history of Scotland until Roman times.

Picts and Romans

In AD80–84 the Roman general **Agricola** sought to add Caledonia – the land that is now Scotland – to the Roman Empire. He defeated the Picts, the native Celtic people, at Mons Graupius, but the Romans never consolidated their victory. Instead, in 142, **Emperor Antonine** built a defensive rampart across the narrowest part of Caledonia, between the rivers Clyde and Forth. Antonine's Wall was soon abandoned and Hadrian's Wall, running across Britain from the Solway in the west to the Tyne in the east, became the frontier between Roman Britain and the Pictish nations until the 5th century. It did not stop the Picts, the Scots of Hibernia (today's Ireland) and the Saxons of the European North Sea coasts from invading Roman Britain in 367. They were repelled, but as the power of Rome waned, the Romans paid a form of tribute to the Picts of the region around Edinburgh to deter them from frontier raids.

Scots, Saxons and Vikings

The people called Scots originated in Ireland and began settling in the less-populated west of Caledonia in the 5th century AD, creating the kingdom of **Dalriada**. Their language was in all probability very like that of the Picts, and their royal families eventually intermarried. At around the same time, Anglo-Saxons began to settle in the southeast of Scotland. Christianity came to Scotland from Ireland, brought by the Irish-Scots missionary St Columba, who founded a religious community on the island of Iona in 563.

Until the 9th century AD, Scots, Picts, and Anglo-Saxons, and also Viking raiders from Scandinavia, fought each other for control of the region. In 843, Kenneth MacAlpin, King of the Scots of Dalriada, conquered the Picts of northern and eastern Scotland to become king of all lands north of the Forth. In 1018, MacAlpin's descendant, Malcolm II, confirmed Scottish rule over the region with the defeat of an Anglo-Saxon army at Carham. By 1032 the frontiers of mainland Scotland stood roughly where they are now. However, Scottish kings exercised no real control over the Highlands, where the clans remained proudly independent.

Above: *Iona Abbey, on a tiny Hebridean island, was founded by the Irish Saint Columba who first brought Christianity to the pagan Scots.*

The Wars of Independence

The Norman kings who ruled England regarded Scotland as part of their domain but by and large left it alone. The Scottish kings were content to avoid conflict with England and concentrated instead on bringing the outlying regions of Scotland under their control. But matters changed with the advent of Edward I of England, who earned the soubriquet 'Hammer of the Scots' for his determination to subjugate Scotland. Scottish incursions south of the border caused Edward to invade Scotland in 1296 in retaliation, triggering the long Wars of Independence.

UP HELLY AA

The Up Helly Aa fire festival, held each January, is a celebration dating from Viking times. The 'Jarl Squad' in full Viking regalia lead a torchlight procession through the Lerwick streets, before the spectacular torching of a full-sized replica longship, and this is followed by a night of drinking, dancing and the fiddle music for which **Shetland** is famous.

William Wallace (1270–1305), immortalized in the Mel Gibson film *Braveheart*, is a near-legendary figure. We first hear of him as a young knight involved in a fight with English soldiers at Lanark in 1297, a year after Edward I's seizure of Edinburgh and conquest of Scotland. According to one version, Wallace was defending a girl, perhaps his wife, who helped him to escape but was herself caught and executed by the Sheriff of Lanark. The vengeful Wallace in turn killed the Sheriff, went on the run and raised a force of freedom fighters who wiped out a large English army at Stirling Bridge and went on to drive the English from most of southern Scotland. However, Wallace's guerrillas were lured into a pitched battle at Falkirk in July 1298 and subsequently scattered. In 1305 he was eventually captured and executed by hanging, drawing and quartering.

Edward's wanton acts of cruelty and violence provoked national resistance, spearheaded by a charismatic commoner, Sir William Wallace, who raised an army from all over Scotland to resist the invaders. He defeated a large English force at Stirling Bridge in September 1297 but his army was destroyed at Falkirk the following year and he was eventually captured and executed.

Robert the Bruce succeeded the Scottish throne and conducted guerrilla warfare against the English. By 1314 he had driven the English from all but one castle, at Stirling. Marching to relieve this last garrison, Edward II was defeated at Bannockburn. The two countries were soon at war again, continuing on and off for three centuries.

When not fighting the English, Scottish kings had to contend with their own rebellious Lowland nobles and the Highland clans. A succession of monarchs succeeded to the throne while still children and the power vacuum was filled by the over-mighty nobility, who ruled as regents and consolidated power into their own hands.

Reformation and Revolt

The Protestant Reformation which reached Scotland in the first half of the 16th century added religious conflict to political rivalries, a condition that was to continue for two centuries. Catholic nobles backed France while the Protestant faction aligned itself with England. By the middle of the 16th century the Protestant party, aided by firebrand reformers like **John Knox**, had taken control of Scottish politics and society. The Catholic Mary, Queen of Scots, was forced to flee Scotland in 1568 and her baby son, crowned James VI, was raised as a Protestant prince. Presbyterianism became the state religion.

On the death of his cousin, Elizabeth I, in 1603, James VI became James I of England. The most competent of the Stuart monarchs, James presided over the longest peace the two countries had yet enjoyed. His son, Charles I, however, tried to impose the episcopalian forms of the Church of England on Scotland, alienating the Presbyterian Scots, while his autocratic ambitions ultimately provoked civil war in England.

The Civil Wars

When civil war broke out in England the Scots stood aside until 1643, when after a series of Royalist victories the English Parliamentarians offered them £30,000 a month to attack the Royalists. The conflict spread throughout Scotland. In 1646, Charles surrendered to the Scots, and the following year the Scottish Parliament switched sides, sending an army to support Charles. A series of disasters followed. The Scots were defeated by the English Parliamentarians at Preston in 1647, and, by 1651, a garrison army under General Monck controlled all of Scotland.

In 1660, on the death of Oliver Cromwell, Charles II was restored to the thrones of England, Scotland and Ireland. Charles was succeeded by his Catholic brother, James VII (II in England) in 1685, against whom there were risings in both Scotland and England, culminating in his overthrow by the Dutch Protestant William of Orange in 1688. Scotland was once again divided, with many of the Highland clans supporting James, or at least prepared to fight on his side in hopes of loot. 'Dutch' William's Secretary of State for Scotland, Sir John Dalrymple, Master of Stair, forced the Highland clans to swear allegiance to William, and made a ruthless example of the MacDonalds of Glencoe when their chief failed to sign the oath in time.

THE GLENCOE MASSACRE

On 13 February 1693, 400 troops of the Earl of Argyll's Regiment of Foot murdered 38 men, women and children of the Maclan MacDonald clan of Glencoe, burning their houses and forcing the survivors to flee. Ostensibly, the MacDonalds were punished for being tardy in taking the oath of allegiance to King William. In fact, Stair intended to make an example of them. The massacre was a little too much even for 17th-century Scotland, and William had to dismiss Stair from office. But when the furore had died down, he was rewarded with the title of earl for his services.

Opposite: *Mary, Queen of Scots, portrayed in stained glass at Glasgow's fine Burrell Collection.*
Below: *Glencoe, scene of an infamous incident in the violent 17th century.*

Union with England

The ceaseless wars of the 17th century had wrecked Scotland's economy, and many of its ruling class saw union with England as the only remedy. When England offered to open its trade to Scots merchants and give Scotland £398,085 and ten shillings in

CHARLES EDWARD STUART

Born and raised in exile at the courts of France and Italy, Charles Edward Stuart was Scots only by descent. His aim was not to free Scotland but with French help to conquer Britain. He was not a successful commander. 'There you go for a damned cowardly Italian,' was the verdict of one of his commanders, Lord Elcho, as he fled the field at Culloden, leaving his defeated followers to the Hanoverian bayonets. After several months as a fugitive with a £30,000 price on his head, he escaped to Skye disguised as the maid of the noblewoman Flora MacDonald, and from there fled to France in September 1746, never to return to Scotland.

return for a Treaty of Union uniting the parliaments of the two countries, while preserving Scotland's unique legal system and guaranteeing the position of the Presbyterian Kirk (church), the Scottish Parliament, by the Treaty of Union of 1707, voted itself out of existence.

England's main motive for union was to prevent the exiled Catholic heirs of James II from using Scotland as a base to reclaim the thrones of both nations. It was not entirely successful. In 1714 the English Queen, Anne, died and George of Hanover, the great-grandson of James I, became king. A year later, an army of Jacobite Highlanders, led by the Earl of Mar, rose for James Edward (later known as 'the Old Pretender'), son of James II, and marched on to Edinburgh.

Jacobite Risings

The rising of 1715 was not a conflict between England and Scotland, nor even between Lowland and Highland Scots, but between Jacobites and Hanoverians. By the time James landed in Scotland, however, indecisive generalship had already lost the initiative, and the rebellion quickly petered out.

In 1745 James's son, Charles Edward Stuart (also known as Bonnie Prince Charlie), tried again. He was at first successful, seizing Edinburgh and marching south.

But this time there was little English support for the Jacobite cause. After marching as far south as Derby, the Highland army was forced to turn back, and on 16 April 1746 was bloodily defeated at Culloden near Inverness.

The Highland Clearances

The final pacification of the Highlands which followed was a brutal, efficient and deliberate act of ethnic cleansing and **cultural genocide**. The Jacobite wounded of Culloden were shot where they lay by the orders of the Hanoverian commander, the Duke of Cumberland. Those later found guilty of rebellion were executed or sent as convict labour to the colonies. Homes were burned, livestock and weapons confiscated, and a determined effort began to destroy the clan system and the Highland way of life. The lands of rebel chiefs were confiscated, the wearing of tartan was forbidden, and even the bagpipes were banned. Yet amazingly enough, within a generation the Highlands had become the recruiting ground for the most fiercely loyal and terrifyingly effective troops ever to fight for the British crown, the kilted regiments of the Highland Brigade, known to their German adversaries during World War I as 'the Ladies from Hell'.

Recruitment was aided by poverty and landlessness. In what later became bitterly known as the Highland Clearances of the late 18th and early 19th centuries, landlords evicted their tenants and their black cattle, the traditional grazing animal of the glens, to make room for more profitable flocks of sheep. Hundreds of thousands left the Highlands for the rapidly growing Scottish cities, or went further away, to the USA, Canada, Australia, New Zealand or South America. The building of the first roads through the Highlands helped to bring them under central control.

Above: *Black houses like these were the traditional homes of Highlanders and islanders well into the 19th and even the 20th century.* **Opposite:** *Culloden Moor, which was the scene of the last stand of Bonnie Prince Charlie's Jacobite Highlanders in 1746.*

HIGHLAND GATHERINGS

The surviving culture of the Highlands is celebrated each year at Highland Gatherings throughout Scotland, where kilted strongmen compete at hammer-hurling, shot-putting and of course tossing the caber. These feats of strength were originally used to pick the mightiest warriors to be the bodyguards of chieftains and kings. They are accompanied by pipe and fiddle music and traditional Highland dancing.

Above: *This tenement building is an example of Glasgow's architecture.*

Industrial Revolution and Social Change

By contrast, Lowland Scotland flourished during the second half of the 18th century, with rapid developments in industry, commerce, and literature. Edinburgh and its university became a centre of learning to rank with the greatest in Europe, and revelled in the soubriquet of the **Athens of the North**. Glasgow became a wealthy centre of commerce with the American colonies, and the manufacturing industry began to grow rapidly. The works of **Robert Burns**, in the second half of the 18th century, and **Sir Walter Scott**, in the first half of the 19th century, rekindled interest in a romanticized Scottish culture.

By the beginning of the 19th century social, political and economic change were transforming Scotland's cities and its countryside. The Industrial Revolution turned Scotland into an overwhelmingly urban society. During the first half of the 19th century, almost 400,000 people moved into the towns of Clydeside, which was rapidly becoming one of the largest manufacturing areas in the world. At the beginning of the 19th century, Glasgow had a population of around 77,000 people. Within two generations their numbers had more than tripled, and by the 1930s it had become one of Britain's biggest cities, with more than a million people. Other cities experienced similar increases, and many of these people lived in the worst urban squalor in Europe. Attempts to improve health, housing and urban infrastructure began only in the second half of the 19th century and continued for more than a century.

THE AGE OF STEAM

James Watt (1736–1819), father of the age of steam, is often credited with having 'invented' the steam engine. In fact stationary steam engines were already in use to pump water from deep mines and quarries. Watt improved these inefficient, clumsy machines, patenting the separate condenser and air pump, the reciprocating and double-stroke engine, the centrifugal governor to regulate engine speed, and also the fuel-saving furnace, making it possible for steam engines to power large ships and locomotives.

HISTORICAL CALENDAR

AD80–84 The Roman invasion of Caledonia.
367 Picts and Scots invade Roman Britain.
5th–6th century AD Roman legions withdraw from Britain. Scots from Ireland settle in western Scotland. Christian missionaries from Ireland establish monasteries in Hebrides.
563 Columba establishes mission on Iona.
843 Kenneth MacAlpin conquers Pictish kingdom to create a kingdom north of the Forth.
9th century Norse Vikings settle the Northern Isles, Caithness, Sutherland and the Hebridean islands.
1018 Malcolm II, King of Scots, defeats Angles of Northumbria at Carham to cement Scottish rule over Lothian.
1296–1328 Edward I and Edward II of England invade

and occupy Scotland. The resistance is led first by William Wallace, then by Robert Bruce.
1297 Battle of Stirling Bridge.
1314 The English are defeated at Bannockburn.
1329 Edward II recognizes Scottish independence.
1507 The first printing press in Edinburgh.
1513 The Scottish army led by James IV is defeated at Flodden.
1603 Union of the Crowns; James VI of Scotland becomes James I of England.
1639–51 Civil Wars, with Scotland divided internally, and Scots armies fighting both for and against Royalists.
1660 Restoration of Charles II.
1688–89 Ousting of James II by William; the fighting in Scotland between Jacobite and Williamite supporters ends in defeat for James.

1707 Treaty of Union abolishes Scottish Parliament.
1715 First Jacobite rising.
1745 Battle of Prestonpans begins second Jacobite rising.
1746 The Jacobites defeated at Culloden.
1801 Population of Scotland stands at 1,608,420.
1846 Railway connects Edinburgh and London.
1890 The Forth Railway Bridge is completed.
1911 Population of Scotland stands at 4,760,904.
1947 The first Edinburgh Festival is held.
1967 Winnie Ewing becomes the first Scottish Nationalist MP.
1979 Apathetic response to referendum on devolution.
1997 Scottish referendum vote to restore Scottish Parliament.
1999 New Scottish Parliament sits for the first time.

Scottish Socialism

Poor living and working conditions provided fertile ground for left-wing ideas, and Scots were prominent in the creation of both the British Labour Party and the trade union movement. The heavy industrial belt around Glasgow was nicknamed 'Red Clydeside' and there was widespread violence between strikers, police and troops during the National Strike of 1926. The worldwide depression of the early 1930s reinforced Scottish socialist and trade unionist beliefs. In the postwar election of 1945, Scottish votes helped sweep a Labour Party government to power at Westminster. Scots once again tipped the balance in Labour's favour in subsequent elections in the 1960s and 1970s.

Below: *The Forth Railway Bridge was a triumph of Victorian engineering in the age of steam.*

Opposite: *Lobster pots line the quayside at Arbroath harbour.*
Below: *North Sea oil changed the face of the northeast of Scotland.*

Towards Home Rule

Demands for home rule for Scotland became much louder in the 1960s and the first Scottish National Party MP, Winnie Ewing, was elected in 1967. In a referendum in 1979, only some 33 per cent voted for the devolution of elected government from London to Edinburgh, but between 1979 and 1997 Scots were alienated by a series of Conservative governments to the extent that in the general election of 1997 the Conservatives won not a single Scottish seat. Also in 1997, a new referendum on devolution made it clear that 'the settled will of the Scottish people' was for devolution, and in 1999 elections were held for the first parliament to sit in Edinburgh in almost three centuries. Scotland entered the 21st century as 'a nation once again'.

GOVERNMENT AND ECONOMY

Scotland's political centre of gravity is well to the left of England's. From 1979 to 1997, when English voters elected a succession of right-wing Conservative governments, Scots voted increasingly for Labour, the Scottish National Party and the Liberal Democrats. The government in London was seen as out of touch with Scotland's needs and wishes, fuelling demands for devolution that had been bubbling under since the 1960s.

In May 1997, the landslide which swept Tony Blair's 'New Labour' government to power was even more marked north of the border, where the Conservative Party failed to hold a single parliamentary seat. New Labour promised a referendum on devolution, the result of which determined that the Scottish people were overwhelmingly in favour of a degree of self-government.

In May 1999, elections were held for the first Scottish Parliament to sit in Edinburgh, Scotland's capital, since 1707. The Labour party, without a governing majority, formed a coalition with the Liberal Democrats.

Today the Scottish Parliament's powers – especially its tax-raising powers – are quite limited, and it remains very much subordinate to the government in London. The Scottish National Party continues to campaign for full independence, and many Scots see the events of 1999 as being the first, irrevocable step along this road.

Devolution gave a tremendous boost to Scotland's self-image, and at the same time the nation's confidence was boosted

by an economic recovery which saw growth in the service and manufacturing sectors and in employment. Unemployment, however, is still a problem in many Scottish communities, rural as well as urban. Over the last 30 years, heavy manufacturing industry has declined while the service sector has expanded.

A major factor in the Scottish (and British) economy since the late 1970s has been the exploitation of the oilfields beneath the North Sea, which brought a boom to Aberdeen, the northeast, Orkney and Shetland. Scottish oil revenue, however, was not husbanded or invested in Scotland, and this unfortunately contributed to both mass unemployment and crippling military spending. North Sea oil is now close to running out and this, together with the decline of the fishing industry, has hit the northeast's local economy hard.

Throughout Scotland, new sectors such as **computing** and **biotechnology** have become more important, and established sectors such as financial services have expanded too. **Tourism** is a major contributor to the economy, but has languished in recent years, with little or no growth in visitor figures.

CASHING IN

Visitors to Scotland are sometimes surprised to find banknotes issued by the Royal Bank of Scotland, the Bank of Scotland and the Clydesdale Bank in circulation. Scotland's currency is the **pound sterling**, as in England, and notes are in the same denominations as those issued by the Bank of England, but the Scottish banks have issued their own notes since 1695. English banknotes are valid north of the border. Scottish notes are generally accepted in England but are harder to exchange outside the UK. When Britain joins the EU's euro zone, Scottish banks may lose the right to print their own banknotes.

THE PEOPLE

In the absence of a distinct Scots language, defining Scottishness is no easy task. Bens and glens, bagpipes, tartan, the kilt, clan surnames, Gaelic, porridge, tossing the caber, haggis and even whisky are symbols of a Scotland that is more 19th-century myth than 21st-century reality. Only a tiny number of Scots actually wear the kilt, even on special occasions. The most common surname, far from beginning with 'Mac-', is Robertson. Oatmeal porridge is far more likely to be found on any American breakfast menu than in its country of origin, and Scots drink more vodka than whisky. And far from living in Highland crofting communities, some nine out of ten Scots are urban dwellers, making Scotland the most 'citified' nation in the European Union.

That said, Scotland has a distinct, and increasingly self-confident, cultural identity. Scots like to imply that their social structure is more egalitarian and meritocratic than that of class-riddled England. For many people, working-class roots are a matter of pride, while the mainly expatriate aristocracy, despite bearing the surnames of the great clan chiefs, are perceived as little more than Anglicized absentee landlords.

The truth is, too, that the Scotland of today is a product of the social and economic changes of the 19th and 20th centuries. During the 19th century, hundreds of thousands of Scots emigrated to the USA, Canada, Australia, New Zealand and South Africa. From the 1840s onward, large numbers of Irish immigrants arrived, fleeing famine and finding ready employment in the mills, mines and shipyards of newly industrializing Scotland. Assimilated into the Scottish identity, their descendants are still here, making up some 20 per cent of the population and with little to distinguish them other than an Irish surname, their traditional support for football clubs such as Celtic or Hibernian, and their fading attachment to the Roman Catholic faith.

MADE IN SCOTLAND

Few peoples can lay claim to so many of the modern **world's great inventions** as can the Scots. Among them:
• banking and bank fraud (both invented by John Law)
• market economics (Adam Smith)
• the steam engine (James Watt)
• the waterproof raincoat (Mackintosh)
• the all-weather highway (Macadam)
• the bolt action rifle (Lee)
• penicillin (Fleming)
• surgical anaesthesia
• the telephone (Alexander Graham Bell)
• television (John Logie Baird)
• radar (Watson Watt)
Strangely enough, one of the discoveries most closely associated with Scotland – **whisky** – was invented not by Scots but by Irish monks.

Later waves of immigrants who have added a distinctive flavour to the Scottish melting pot include the large numbers of Italians who arrived in the late 19th and early 20th centuries, while in the second half of the 20th century significant numbers of people came to Scotland from Commonwealth countries such as Hong Kong, Bangladesh, India and Pakistan, to the extent that there will soon be more mother-tongue Urdu speakers in Scotland than native Gaelic speakers.

Scots tend to be keenly aware of their local loyalties; you can travel from Glasgow to Edinburgh in less time than it takes to cross London, but natives feel that the two are as different as New York and Los Angeles. Life in the Highlands and Isles is very different from life in the big cities of the Lowlands. And Orcadians and Shetlanders, whose descent may be more Norse than Scots, stand somewhat aloof from the mainland.

Language

Gaelic has not been the majority language of Scotland for around 1000 years, and is now spoken by only some one per cent of Scots, most living in the Western Isles. **Scots**, as a tongue akin to but significantly different from English, was abandoned by the ruling class after the Union of 1707, though it persisted as a working-class dialect well into the 19th century, especially in the rural southwest and northeast. Robert Burns wrote in it, and from the early 20th century, writers such as Lewis Grassic Gibbon and Hugh MacDiarmid sought to revive it as a literary medium. Today, you may ask a question in standard English and be understood by any Scot. Scotland has, however, a rich and varied brew of **regional accents and dialects**, and you may not find the response to your question so readily comprehensible.

> **GAME OF THE NAME**
>
> Scots seem to delight in catching the visitor out with names whose spelling seems to bear no resemblance to their pronunciation. Some examples include surnames such as Colquhoun (pronounced Cahoon), Urquhart (pronounced Urkart), Menzies (Mingus), Farquahar (Farker), and Dalziel (Diyell).

Opposite: *A kilted piper in full Highland dress making music at Glencoe.*
Below: *Energetic Highland dancers go through their paces at the Lochearnhead Highland Gathering.*

Opposite: *Monument to Sir Walter Scott dominates Edinburgh's Princes Street.*
Below: *Church at Iona, still a place of pilgrimage for Scottish Christians of all denominations.*

Religion

Religion in Scotland spans greater extremes than any other part of the United Kingdom except Northern Ireland. Traditionally, the established Church (or Kirk) of Scotland is **Presbyterian**, dispensing with archbishops, bishops and the other appointed prelates of the Church of England. The monarch is indeed its titular head, but its ruling body is the General Assembly, elected by the elders of each parish, which in turn elects its own Moderator for a fixed term. The Kirk and its ministers played an enormously important role in Scotland's history from the 16th century onward, but its temporal and spiritual power has waned in a more secular era. The Episcopalian Church of Scotland, which is similar in structure to the Church of England, has a smaller following, and there are also a number of smaller, more severely Presbyterian churches such as the United Free Church of Scotland. A substantially larger proportion of Scots – as many as one in five, many of Irish and Italian descent – are Roman Catholic. There are also small Jewish communities, mainly in larger cities, where a few mosques and temples testify to the presence of Muslim, Sikh and Hindu minorities.

Writers, Philosophers and Poets

Scotland's earliest literature, whether in Gaelic, medieval Scots or English, grew from an **oral tradition** of ballads and songs, usually telling of the great warlike feats of

kings and chieftains. The 15th century was a golden age for Scottish poets – among them James I himself, and also Robert Henryson, whose many poems based on myths and fables make him medieval Scotland's closest rival to his English near-contemporary, Geoffrey Chaucer.

The great religious en-
thusiasm for literacy, which
swept through Scotland as
a result of the Protestant
Reformation, created the first
society in history in which
reading and writing were
skills no longer confined to a
tiny elite but available to all.

The 18th century was the
era of **Allan Ramsay**, the
Edinburgh bookseller, Jacobite,
satirist and playwright who
wrote in both standard English
and the Scots vernacular. It
was, too, the time of the
'Scottish Enlightenment', when
Edinburgh became known as
the 'Athens of the North' and
its colleges produced figures
such as the atheist and logician

David Hume, the moral philosopher Adam Ferguson and
the historian William Robertson. Dr Samuel Johnson's
sidekick and biographer, James Boswell, though he spent
much of his life outside Scotland, was another product of
this period, as was the prodigy Robert Fergusson who
in his tragically short career celebrated the street-life of
18th-century Edinburgh to great acclaim. But the second
half of the century belongs to the most famous Scot of all,
Robert Burns, whose poems and songs breathed new
literary life into vernacular Scots.

Sir Walter Scott was the greatest literary figure of
the early 19th century, celebrating and romanticizing
Scotland's past. Later in the century **Robert Louis
Stevenson** turned out historical romances, thrillers and
chillers which have inspired numerous film versions.
Though there is nothing uniquely Scots in the work of Sir
Arthur Conan Doyle, the world's most famous detective,
Sherlock Holmes, was inspired by Dr Joseph Bell of
Edinburgh, who virtually invented forensic science.

ON LOAN

The poet **Allan Ramsay**
(1684–1758), a wigmaker
turned bookseller, turned his
hand to writing essays and
poetry both in standard
English and the Scottish
vernacular. He scandalized
Edinburgh by establishing
Britain's first circulating
library, lending the latest
books and plays from London
for tuppence a night at a
time when religious works
were virtually the only writing
approved by the powerful
Kirk, and by campaigning for
the legalizing of the theatre
in Edinburgh, where the
church frowned on such
frivolity. The theatre was
eventually licensed in 1764,
six years after Ramsay's death.

Above: *Edinburgh's streets are alive with performers of all sorts during the famous annual arts festival in August.*

TRAVELLER'S TALES

Robert Louis Stevenson (1850–1894) wrote dozens of travel books, historical romances and adventure tales that remain popular today – especially *Treasure Island* (1883) which still inspires film versions and retellings, as does *The Strange Case of Dr Jekyll and Mr Hyde* (1886), the story of a respectable doctor who meddles with drugs and releases his evil, uncontrollable alter ego. A world traveller and lifelong sufferer from tuberculosis, Stevenson made his final home in Samoa, where he died and is buried.

At the turn of the 19th century, J M Barrie, best known now for the creation of *Peter Pan*, was the leading light of the 'Kailyard School' of writers who sentimentalized Scottish working-class life in country and city and whose work has not aged well. By the 1920s, writers such as Hugh MacDiarmid were harnessing literature to a kind of left-leaning cultural nationalism, in a conscious attempt to revive or create a distinctively Scottish literary and political culture. Others who drove this Scottish cultural renaissance well into the second half of the century included the poets Sorley MacLean and Norman MacCaig, the novelist Lewis Grassic Gibbon , Neil M Gunn and Hamish Henderson, a poet and musician.

More recently acclaimed Scottish writers include the novelists James Kelman, winner of the Booker Prize in 1994 for *How Late it Was, How Late*, as well as A L Kennedy, Alasdair Gray, Irvine Welsh, and Iain Banks.

Music and Song

Scotland is indeed a land of music and song, from the warlike marches and plaintive laments of the bagpipes to the foot-tapping jigs and reels of traditional fiddle music, and from the ballads of the medieval minstrels to the praise-poems of Gaelic bards who were part of every clan chief's household.

The **pipes** are most commonly associated with the kilted pipe bands of the Highland regiments, and with marching bands wherever in the world Scots have settled. Purists say these tunes for massed pipers are no better than pop music, and that the true *ceol mor* (the great music) of the solo *piobaireachd* (pibroch) piper, unique to Scotland, is the highest form of the art. Gaelic songs, often celebrating love and loss, are usually sung unaccompanied or to the accompaniment of the small harp called the **clarsach**, another typical instrument of the Celtic world of both Scotland and Ireland.

In Lowland Scotland, an equally ancient tradition is that of the **ballad**, telling tales of battle, heroism, love or revenge. Many of these come from the debatable land of the border country, where the bloody deeds of 'reivers' like the Kers, Maxwells, Nixons and Armstrongs, who defied the laws of Edinburgh and London, provided plentiful material for balladeers.

Jigs and reels from all over the Lowlands, originally composed for the fiddle, have survived as Scottish country dance music (and are the inspiration for much of the country music of the United States).

Like so much of Scottish culture, **traditional music** was debased into music-hall entertainment through the 19th and well into the second half of the 20th century. The great Harry Lauder, whose interpretation of songs by Burns and others earned him a knighthood, was followed by dozens of imitators. The diminutive, kilted Andy Stewart came to fame performing *Donald, where's yer troosers*, and Jimmy Shand and his band of accordion players performed medleys of reels and strathspeys.

> **BY ROYAL APPOINTMENT**
>
> Born in Crail in 1710, **James Oswald** went on to become court composer to King George III and master of Knebworth House and its estates, outside London. He started his career as a dancing master in Dunfermline, composed fiddle music in Edinburgh, and was the first anthologizer of Scottish folk tunes, publishing several collections of songs between 1745 and his death in 1769. You can hear some of his songs on *Colin's Kisses: The Music of James Oswald* (Linn Records, 1999).

Below: *Since the 1970s, Scottish pub life has tended to move outdoors.*

UNOFFICIAL ANTHEM

Flower of Scotland, the ballad which celebrates the victories of Bruce and Wallace over 'proud Edward's armies' in the Wars of Independence, has become Scotland's un-official national anthem, belted out by the 'Tartan Army' of Scottish football supporters at international games and other mass events. Whether it will ever enjoy official status as the anthem of an independent Scotland is another matter. It is in fact neither ancient, nor the work of a Scot – it was written in 1968 by **Roy Williamson**, an Englishman and founder of the folk group, The Corries.

Opposite: *Glasgow's Art Gallery and Museum is one of Scotland's finest.*
Below: *The reconstructed hull of a Viking longship reveals similarities to modern fishing vessels.*

But through the second half of the 20th century, more authentic Scottish traditional music enjoyed a strong revival, first in the 1960s, with the saccharine songs of Robin Hall and Jimmie MacGregor and their television show, the White Heather Club, and bands like The Corries. More recently, bands like Runrig and Jock Tamson's Bairns have fused traditional music with a diversity of influences to create a new, distinctively Scottish form of 'world music'.

Scotland has also produced its fair share of world-class rock and pop bands and performers during the last three decades, ranging from Maggie Bell to Stone the Crows, the Sensational Alex Harvey Band, the funk-rock Average White Band, the art-college punk of The Rezillos, the Bay City Rollers, Annie Lennox, Deacon Blue, Simple Minds, Texas, and Lloyd Cole and The Commotions, to name but a few.

Visual Arts

The Scots, Picts and Vikings of the early centuries of Scottish history have left remarkable works of crafts-manship, in the form of gold and silver brooches, neck and arm rings and other **jewellery**. Little of the rich religious ornamentation of abbeys, cathedrals and monasteries survived the zeal of the Protestant reformers or the wars of the 16th and 17th centuries, but **carvings**

in wood and stone from religious, secular and royal buildings can be seen in Scotland's major museums, as can tapestries and fine furniture.

The more secure world of the later 18th century saw a flowering in the visual arts as well as in literature, when portraitists Allan Ramsay and Henry Raeburn painted the cream of Scottish society and its intelligentsia. Symbolic of this new era of the 'Scottish Enlightenment' was the **architecture** of Edinburgh's gracious New Town, which was planned by James Craig and executed by the Adam brothers. During the 19th century, Alexander Thomson designed several of Glasgow's great commercial and municipal buildings, while Charles Rennie Mackintosh's brilliance in all aspects of design earned him a worldwide reputation.

Sport and Recreation

Football (soccer) is something of a **national obsession** and Scotland supports more than its fair share of teams. Rivalry is especially fierce between the 'Old Firm' Glasgow clubs, Celtic and Rangers, but Scots bury all regional hatchets when the national team goes abroad, and especially when Scotland meets England in international contests. Rugby is not as popular as in England, though it has a strong regional following in Edinburgh and the Borders.

Participatory sports include **golf** – invented in Scotland and played with enthusiasm on hundreds of local courses as well as on world-class links such as Gleneagles, St Andrews, Troon or Carnoustie – skiing,

Right: *Eilean Donan, the most often filmed and photographed Scottish castle.*
Opposite: *Fresh lobster is a popular item on many seafood menus.*

athletics and a wide range of watersports from dinghy, yacht and board sailing to whitewater canoeing. **Hill walking** and mountaineering are, naturally, also very popular. 'Traditional' Highland sports such as **tossing the caber** are really a 19th-century invention, but can be seen during various Highland events in summer.

Film

Scotland's hills, glens and castles have been the backdrop to movies as diverse as *Chariots of Fire, Highlander, Local Hero, Rob Roy, Braveheart* (though ironically, much of this saga of the freedom fighter William Wallace was shot in Ireland) and *The World is Not Enough*, while the landscapes of Deeside were the setting for *Mrs Brown*.

Glasgow is the backdrop for films such as *Gregory's Girl* and its 1999 sequel, *Gregory's Two Girls*, and also for *Trainspotting* – set in Edinburgh but made in Glasgow – and for Ken Loach's *Carla's Song, Small Faces*, and *Orphans*. Released in late 1999, Scottish director Lynne Ramsay's film about life on a Glasgow housing estate, *Ratcatcher*, won immediate acclaim.

Food and drink

The traditional diet of both Lowland and Highland Scots was a healthy one, rich in fibre and complex vegetable proteins from oats, barley and pulses, relatively low in fat and red meat and high in oily fish such as herring. The Industrial Revolution of the 19th century changed all that, and for more than a century the national diet was a lethal mix of animal fats, starch and sugar. Add the world's highest per capita consumption of sugar, a strong predilection for tea, tobacco and alcohol and it is not surprising that Scotland for many years had record levels of heart disease and tooth decay. The fish and chip shop or 'chipper' is still a national institution, serving not just deep-fried fish and chips but deep-fried meat pies, black and white puddings, haggis, sausage, deep-fried pizza and even deep-fried Mars bars.

However, Scottish catering has changed with the times. Scots chefs have created a distinctively Scottish take on new cuisine, using Scotland's own superb produce – lamb, beef, game such as pheasant, grouse and venison, and fine seafood from the North Sea and Atlantic coasts. The list of acclaimed **new restaurants**, not just in major cities, but in the remotest parts of the Highlands, gets longer each year.

Scotland produces no wines of its own, but wines of all qualities are imported from Europe and the New World and are reasonably priced. Scottish brewing has improved, too, over the last two decades, with a much larger range of beers – mostly **dark ales** – available on draught and in the bottle.

SCOTCH WHISKY

Many whiskies can be found, ranging from generic super-market brands to staggeringly expensive limited edition malts made for export to the Asian markets. Scotch whisky is made from malted barley dried over an open fire, giving a distinctive **smoky flavour**. Taste and colour vary, from the dark, peaty malt whiskies of Islay and Jura to the pale, gold malts of the northeast. Blended whiskies are made by combining malt distillate with neutral spirits, and as a rule the more malt used, the better the blend. Pure malt whiskies are just what the name implies.

2
Edinburgh

In the 7th century, the Angles of Northumbria built a fort atop **Castle Rock**, a steep-sided, 100m (328ft) crag, which they named Edinburgh (Edwin's Fort). Scotland's capital stands on the south shore of the **Firth of Forth**, hemmed in to the south by the rolling **Pentland Hills**. Edinburgh Castle, on its crag, is visible from all over the city, with the Old Town – the core of the medieval city – huddled around and below. A skyline bristling with church steeples reflects a history dominated by deep religious conviction; the domes of great public buildings of the 18th and 19th centuries highlight the city's role as a centre of learning and culture. Another landmark, the peak of **Arthur's Seat**, looms above the city.

Edinburgh is a city of great variety, with medieval streets, castles and palaces, Georgian terraces, high culture and dusk-till-dawn nightlife. 'Auld Reekie' (Old Smoky), as Edinburgh was nicknamed, embodies two cities – the Old Town, around and beneath Edinburgh Castle, and the New Town, designed during the 18th century.

Westward, along the south shore of the Firth of Forth, are a number of sights worth seeing, with fascinating historic associations. This was once the northern limit of the Roman Empire, and archaeologists have made new discoveries at the Roman fortress site at Cramond, just to the west of Edinburgh. Linlithgow, with its haunting ruined palace, was for centuries the home of Scottish monarchs, while near South Queensferry, in the shadow of the mighty Forth bridges, are the stately homes of aristocratic Scottish families.

DON'T MISS

*** Edinburgh Castle:
Edinburgh's most famous and prominent landmark.
*** Museum of Scotland:
new museum with collections from prehistory to present.
** Scott Monument:
a monument to a great 19th-century author.
** Hopetoun House:
one of the finest of Scotland's stately homes.
** Dynamic Earth:
exciting and imaginative visitor attraction brings geology to life.

Opposite: *Edinburgh Castle, pictured from Princes Street Gardens.*

THE ROYAL MILE

The Royal Mile – a sequence of streets which merge into
each other – runs between Edinburgh Castle and the
Palace of Holyroodhouse. Every inch of it, and almost
every building, has an interesting story to tell – uncanny,
gory, tragic or romantic.

Edinburgh Castle ***

Edinburgh Castle is the most potent symbol of the
city and its past. From its ramparts there are superb
panoramic views. The entrance is flanked by statues of
Robert the Bruce and William Wallace. Within the castle
is the Crown Room, housing the crown, sword and
sceptre of the kings and queens of Scotland, and also
the Stone of Destiny. The **royal apartments** include
the Queen's Bedchamber, which was the birthplace of
James VI and I. Within the castle vaults, pride of place
goes to the mighty **Mons Meg**, an enormous cannon
made in 1449. The west wing of the castle houses the

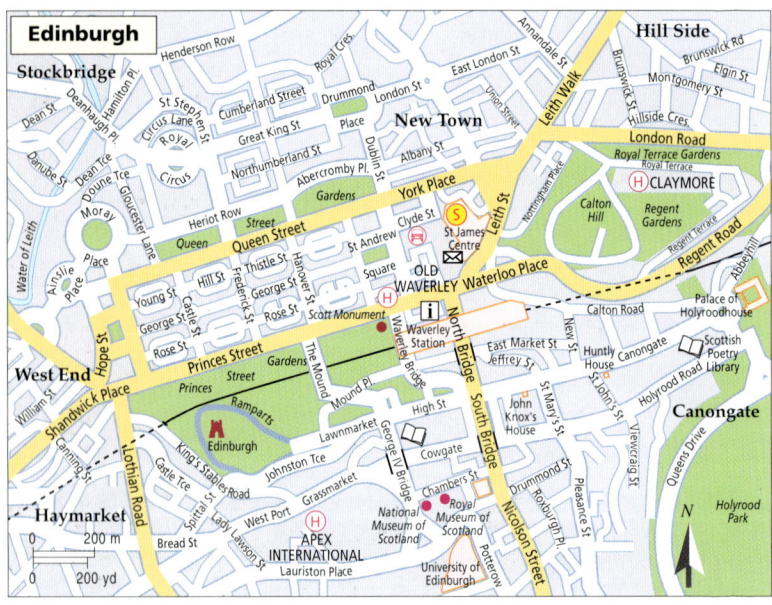

Scottish United Services Museum, a fine collection of regimental honours.

Scotch Whisky Heritage Centre **

At 354 Castlehill, the Scotch Whisky Heritage Centre (open daily, 10:00–17:30) is home to 300 years of Scotch whisky history. Sample all the blended and single malt whiskies distilled in Scotland.

Above: *Scotch Whisky Heritage Centre, home to over 300 years of Scotch whisky history.*

Outlook Tower and Camera Obscura **

On the north side of Castlehill, at the corner of Ramsay Lane, the Outlook Tower and Camera Obscura were built in the 19th century. The lens and mirror provide a **panorama of Edinburgh**, projected into the darkened chamber. Open daily; hours vary.

Gladstone's Land **

Gladstone's Land, a six-storey 17th-century merchant's home and shop which has been restored by the National Trust for Scotland, was the home of the merchant Thomas Gledstanes, or Gladstone (an ancestor of the 19th-century Prime Minister, William Ewart Gladstone). Open from 1 April to 31 October; times vary.

Lady Stair's House (Writers' Museum) **

Lady Stair's House, situated on Lady Stair's Close, next to Gladstone's Land, is a 17th-century townhouse crammed with the memorabilia of three of Scotland's greatest writers, namely Robert Burns, Sir Walter Scott and Robert Louis Stevenson.

Lady Stair, widow of John Dalrymple, first Earl of Stair (1648–1707), bought the house in 1719 and lived here until her death 12 years later. Open Monday–Saturday, and Sunday afternoon during the Edinburgh Festival.

HOIST WITH HIS OWN PETARD

At the corner of Edinburgh's Bank Street and the Lawnmarket, **Deacon Brodie's** is a venerable **pub** with villainous associations, where Deacon William Brodie, respectable citizen, skilled cabinet-maker and Town Councillor by day, robber and burglar by night, is claimed to have planned his exploits. Brodie was betrayed by one of his accomplices after the particularly daring burglary of the General Excise Office, fled to Amsterdam, but was caught, convicted, and hanged on a gallows that, ironically, was of his own design.

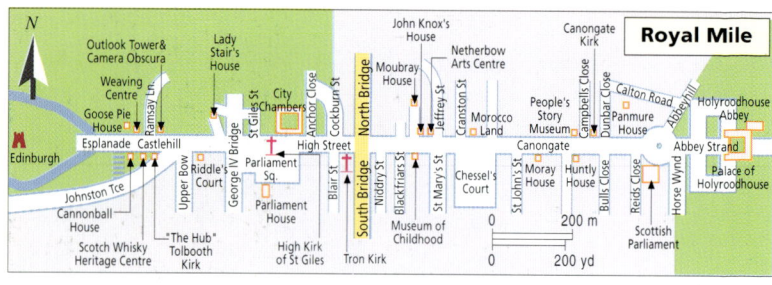

High Kirk (St Giles Cathedral) **

On Parliament Square, the High Kirk (formerly St Giles Cathedral) is Edinburgh's most imposing church, dating from 1120. Burnt during an English raid in 1385, the church was rebuilt and expanded, and in 1460 it was again enlarged. In 1495 the crown spire was added. A statue of the 16th-century reformer **John Knox** stands just within the main entrance. Outside it stands the Mercat (Market) Cross, dating from 1885, with part of the original 14th-century cross built into its shaft.

Edinburgh City Chambers *

Opposite the Cross, on the northern side of the Lawnmarket, is the impressive **arcaded façade** of the Edinburgh City Chambers, which was designed by John Adam and completed in 1761. In 1811 it was taken over by the Town Council and is now the meeting place of the City of Edinburgh Council.

Below right: *Edinburgh's High Kirk, formerly called St Giles Cathedral, is the Scottish capital's most imposing church.*

HEAVEN ON EARTH

The towering, brooding figure of **John Knox**, father of the Reformation in Scotland, still casts a long, dour shadow. Knox was a disciple of the radical reformer John Calvin (Jean Cauvin) of Geneva. He and his followers utterly opposed the forms of the Catholic faith, replacing them with a sterner, puritanical Protestantism in which churches were stripped of all decoration and religion of its priestly ceremony. Knox's aim was to create a **Protestant theocracy** in Scotland, and from his pulpit he became a power to be reckoned with.

Tron Kirk **

Founded in 1637, the Tron takes its name from the **weighing scales** which stood here in medieval times and into the 18th century. It has a well-preserved hammer beam roof.

Museum of Childhood *

Five galleries are crammed with toys and games from all over the world. In the era of Nintendo, Sega and personal computer games, the toys and games of decades as recent as the 1950s and 60s look quaintly obsolete. (Open Monday–Friday, and also Sundays during the Edinburgh Festival; hours vary).

John Knox House **

At 43/45 High Street, this historic townhouse dates from the mid-15th century. John Knox is said to have died here in 1572. The house was extensively restored in 1953. Open Monday–Saturday, 10:00–17:00.

Above: *The John Knox House, originally built in the 15th century and restored in 1953.*

People's Story Museum (Canongate Tolbooth) **

Built in 1591, this building on the Canongate was not only customs house, but also council house, courtroom, prison and place of execution. Today it houses the People's Story Museum, telling **Edinburgh's story** with the aid of sights, sounds and smells from the past. The Tolbooth is decorated with the coat of arms of the burgh, a stag's head bearing a cross between its antlers. Open Monday–Saturday 10:00–17:00, plus Sunday afternoon during the Edinburgh Festival.

Huntly House Museum **

Opposite the Tolbooth, Huntly House, which was built in 1570, houses a fine collection of Edinburgh **crystal and silverware**. Pride of place is given to the National Covenant, a petition signed by Presbyterian nobles and commoners opposing Charles I's attempt in 1638 to impose bishops on the Scottish Kirk. Open from Monday to Saturday 10:00–17:00, plus Sunday afternoon during the Edinburgh Festival.

ARTHUR'S SEAT

Geologically, Arthur's Seat is the relic of a small volcano which erupted around 325 million years ago. The hill's connection with the mythical King Arthur is tenuous. Edinburgh during the 5th century was settled by British refugees from the ruin of Roman Britain. The Roman-British leader on which the Arthurian legends are based may have ruled at around the same time, so perhaps the name came from them. More likely, it was invented by some medieval romantic.

Above: *Holyroodhouse has been Edinburgh's royal palace since the 12th century, but its towers and turrets date from the 16th and 17th centuries.*

THE MAIDEN

One of the more gruesome highlights of the Museum of Scotland is the Maiden, the Scottish forerunner of the French Revolutionary guillotine; an interactive computer display shows how it worked. Grim though it is, the Maiden was, like the guillotine, actually intended to be more merciful than the executioner's axe. Unlike the headsman, the Maiden never missed, guaranteeing its victims a rapid demise.

Palace of Holyroodhouse and Holyrood Abbey ***

Holyroodhouse, at the foot of the Canongate, was the guesthouse of the **Augustinian Abbey**, founded by David I in 1128, and was gradually transformed into a residence fit for royalty. The oldest part is the northern tower dating from between 1528 and 1533. Mary, Queen of Scots, made her home in this tower when she returned as a young widow to Scotland.

The rest of the palace was built between 1671 and 1676, with the addition of a second four-turreted tower. A low, single-storey front connects the two towers, and a Classical columned gateway leads within to an elegant arcaded courtyard.

Inside the palace, the main attraction is the **Picture Gallery**, lined with portraits commissioned by Charles II from the Dutch painter Jacob de Wit (1649–81).

Adjoining the northeastern corner of the palace, Holyrood Abbey is probably Edinburgh's most **picturesque ruin**. It flourished under royal patronage until the Reformation, but during the violence that accompanied the overthrow of James II in 1688–89 it was severely damaged.

Dynamic Earth ***
Interactive video technology unveils the secrets of the world's geology in this new visitor attraction situated on Holyrood Road, about 400m (440yd) from the Palace of Holyroodhouse. Open daily.

Arthur's Seat **
The 251m (823ft) summit offers superb views of Edinburgh and the surrounding countryside from the Pentland Hills to the shores of Fife, and inland to The Ochils. The hill is surrounded by the 259ha (640-acre) Holyrood Park. The paths are well maintained.

THE GRASSMARKET AND THE UNIVERSITY AREA
Situated to the south of Castle Rock, the Grassmarket, which in medieval times was the city's produce market, is a **picturesque district** which consists of cobbled streets and old-fashioned stone buildings, pubs and boutiques. George IV Bridge, running in a southerly direction from the High Street, leads to the University of Edinburgh campus around George Square and Chambers Street, and to two of Scotland's finest museums (*see* page 38).

Greyfriars Bobby *
This rather twee **life-sized monument** located at the junction of George IV Bridge and Candlemaker Row immortalizes the **Skye terrier** who, after the death in 1858 of his master, Police Constable John Gray, stood guard over his grave in the nearby Kirkyard for 14 years until his own death, when a public subscription paid for his statue.

Greyfriars Kirkyard *
On the west side of Candlemaker Row, the first kirk on this site was dedicated in 1620. The Kirk and Kirkyard stand on the site of a Franciscan friary built in the 15th century. Sacked by Cromwell's troops in 1650, the church was rebuilt in 1721 but burned down in 1845. The present building dates from the mid-19th century, and was again extensively restored in 1938.

RINGING THE CHANGES

Born in Edinburgh, **Alexander Graham Bell** (1847–1922) emigrated to the United States at the age of 23. Only five years later, on 2 June 1875, he made the world's first telephone call. The rest is history. A replica of his original telephone is displayed in the Innovators section of the Museum of Scotland.

Below: *The Grassmarket is a picturesque quarter with cobbled streets and old-fashioned stone buildings overlooked by the castle.*

Right: *The annual Tattoo at Edinburgh Castle is a spectacular celebration of the martial virtues of Scotland's kilted regiments.* **Opposite:** *Calton Hill's monuments include an imitation of the Parthenon of ancient Athens.*

Museum of Scotland ***

This award-winning modern building opened in 1998. Its superb, brilliantly laid-out collection illustrating every aspect of Scotland's past covers seven floors, ascending in chronological order from the basement (Level 0). Imaginatively displayed exhibits range from wonderful Iron Age gold brooches and arm rings to the hoard of Roman silver found at Traprain Law, and the Roman statue of a lioness found in the River Almond at Cramond. The first floor highlights the creation of the **Kingdom of the Scots**, with displays of tools and weapons, including the huge two-handed swords known as claymores (from the Gaelic, meaning 'big sword'); they make the much shorter, basket-hilted Highland broadsword, also called the claymore, look like a toy. The exhibits on the third floor of the museum highlight Scotland's transformation from medieval times through to the Union with England in 1707. The fourth and fifth floors cover the Industrial Revolution, and also Scotland in the heyday of the British Empire; and the sixth floor takes you right up to the present day. Open daily except Christmas Day; hours vary.

Royal Museum of Scotland **

Connected to the Museum of Scotland by a walkway, the Royal Museum is a striking Victorian building with an enormous glass-roofed atrium and displays on its mezzanine floors. Highlights include the museum's **science and industry** section, with its good collection of working model steam engines, including the **world's oldest locomotive** – George Stephenson's Rocket – and the **world's oldest glider**. The museum is open daily except Christmas Day; opening hours vary.

Old College *

Edinburgh University Old College occupies the entire block bounded by Chambers Street, South Bridge, West and South College streets. Begun in 1789 and completed between 1817 and 1824, the Talbot Rice Art Gallery inside houses the University's permanent **Torrie Collection** (mainly of 17th-century Dutch and Flemish painters). Open Tuesday–Saturday, 10:00–17:00.

CALTON HILL

Calton Hill, looming 100m (328ft) above the east end of Princes Street, is crowned with monuments, including the columns of a 19th-century folly, the **National Monument**. Inspired by Edinburgh's 18th-century soubriquet, the architect, Charles Robert Cockerell (1788–1863), meant this imitation of the Parthenon to be the crowning glory of the 'Athens of the North'. Intended as a monument to the Scottish dead of the Napoleonic Wars, it was never completed.

Old and New Observatory *

The Old Observatory, built in 1776, and New Observatory, built in 1818, stand side by side at the top of Calton Hill. Open daily; hours vary.

Dugald Stewart Monument *

This eight-columned Doric pavilion (1831) commemorates Dugald Stewart (1753–1828), professor of moral philosophy at Edinburgh University.

IN THE PICTURE

Sir Henry Raeburn (1756–1823) is sometimes called 'the Scottish Reynolds' after his contemporary and tutor, Sir Joshua Reynolds, the great English portraitist. He began painting miniature portraits of his friends at the age of 16, studied painting in Rome and from his return to Edinburgh in 1787 until his death was the most fashionable **portraitist** in Scotland, an associate of the wealthy, aristocratic and famous, and captured in paint many of his notable Scottish contemporaries. A founder of the Royal Scottish Academy, he was knighted in 1822.

Nelson Monument *

This **lighthouse-like tower** was built in 1815 and rises to a turret which allows superb views of the entire city and its surroundings. Closed Sundays.

General Register House *

The elegantly proportioned General Register House, which occupies the north side of Waterloo Place, is guarded by an equestrian statue of the Duke of Wellington. Designed by Robert Adam in 1852, it houses the Scottish Record Office and the Scottish national archives. Open Monday–Friday, 09:00–16:45.

PRINCES STREET

Princes Street is Edinburgh's busiest **shopping** street, and although the architectural mishaps of the second half of the 20th century mar its original gracious appearance it still has sights worth seeing. The attractively landscaped park, **Princes Street Gardens**, runs along the south side of Princes Street for almost its entire length.

Royal Scottish Academy ***

The Royal Scottish Academy (RSA), on the corner of Princes Street and the Mound (entrance on Princes Street), is a **Greek Revival** building built in 1822–26. It houses exhibitions of contemporary Scottish artists year-round. It also hosts an annual Summer Exhibition, timed well to coincide with the Edinburgh International Festival. Open Monday–Saturday 10:00–17:00, Sunday 14:00–17:00.

National Gallery of Scotland ***

Just south of the RSA, the National Gallery of Scotland is rated as one of the finest smaller art museums in Europe. Its collection includes works by Constable, El Greco, Raphael, Rembrandt, Titian, Velazquez, Van

Below: *Princes Street, the thoroughfare which separates the Old Town from modern Edinburgh.*

Gogh and Gauguin, and by
Scottish masters, notably Sir
Henry Raeburn. Open from
Monday to Saturday 10:00–
17:00, Sunday 14:00–17:00.

Scott Monument **

In East Princes Street Gardens,
the 60m (200ft) Gothic stone
spire of the Scott Monument,
built between 1840 and 1846,
is adorned by a statue of **Sir
Walter Scott** and 64 statuettes,
each representing a character
from one of his novels.

THE NEW TOWN

Edinburgh's New Town, a rectangle of Georgian and
Regency streets that begins north of Princes Street, is one
of the first and finest examples of town planning in
Europe. Compared with the Old Town, which grew hap-
hazardly, the New Town is a model of orderly design.
First planned in 1767, the New Town was initially
bounded by Princes Street in the south and Queen Street
in the north, with George Street running through its
centre. **Garden squares** stand at each end of George
Street – Charlotte Square at the western end and St
Andrew Square at the eastern end.

Melville Monument *

On St Andrew Square, the 37m (121ft) column of the
Melville Monument is a prominent landmark, atop which
stands a statue of **Henry Dundas**, first Viscount Melville
(1724–1811). The monument was erected in 1823.

Scottish National Portrait Gallery **

Built in 1885–90, in French Gothic style, the gallery was
the gift of J R Finlay, proprietor of *The Scotsman*,
Scotland's national newspaper, and contains an exten-
sive collection of portraits of influential Scots from the

Above: *The gardens of
Charlotte Square are an
elegant complement to the
gracious Georgian build-
ings of George Street.*

RULE BRITANNIA

The port of Leith, a couple of
miles from the city centre on
the shores of the Firth of
Forth, is undergoing a 21st-
century transformation from
run-down dockland to
vibrant **waterfront** district.
The Shore is the heart of
the newly trendy Leith
waterfront, with smart bars,
gourmet restaurants, chic
shops and desirable apartments overlooking the water.
Permanently moored at
Ocean Drive, Leith's new
waterfront complex is
the Royal Yacht **Britannia**,
which carried the royal family
around the world from the
1950s until the 1990s.

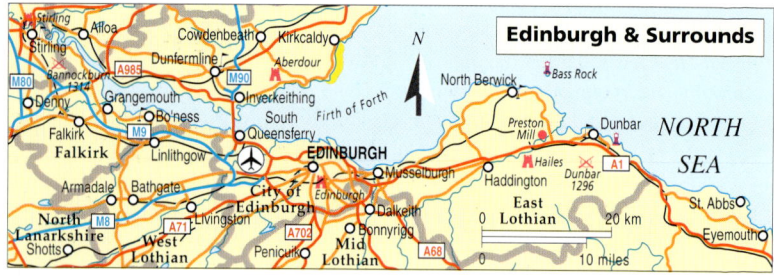

Above: *The Georgian House on Charlotte Street is one of the finest surviving examples of New Town architecture.*

FORTH VALLEY ROUTE

This is a short journey of 62km (39 miles) from Edinburgh through South Queensferry on the south shore of the Firth, past two elegant mansions, Dalmeny House and Hopetoun House, and into Scotland's 19th-century industrial heartland. From here you can take a boat trip on the Union Canal or ride a steam train on the Bo'ness and Kinnell Steam Railway.

18th century onward, including a number by Raeburn and Ramsay. Open Monday–Saturday 10:00–17:00, Sunday 14:00–17:00; extended hours during the Festival.

Georgian House **

Designed by the Edinburgh-educated Robert Adam (1728–92), Charlotte Square is one of the most harmonious examples of European architecture of that era. This gracious building on the north side of the square has been restored and furnished with period pieces.

West Register House **

The west of Charlotte Square is dominated by the splendid dome of the West Register House. Originally St George's Church, built in 1811, it contains the overspill from the Scottish Record Office at the General Register House on Princes Street, mainly 19th- and 20th-century documents.

The Dean Gallery – the Paolozzi Collection ***

On Belford Road, this is Edinburgh's newest gallery, opened in May 1999, with a major collection of **Surrealist art** and a collection of work by Edinburgh-born sculptor and muralist **Sir Eduardo Paolozzi**. Open daily.

Scottish National Gallery of Modern Art ***

On Belford Road, opposite the Dean Gallery, this is Scotland's finest modern art collection, with works by Matisse, Picasso, Lucien Freud and Henry Moore as well as Scottish artists. Open Monday–Saturday 10:00–17:00, Sunday 14:00–17:00.

Royal Botanic Garden ***

The Royal Botanic Garden boasts the **world's largest collection of rhododendrons** (best seen as a marvellous blaze of reds, pinks and purples when they flower in April and May) and a famous **rock garden**. The **Chinese garden** contains the largest collection of Chinese flora outside China itself. In the huge climate-controlled glasshouses exotic plants are displayed in 11 different climate zones, ranging from desert to rainforest. The Royal Botanic Garden is open daily except Christmas Day and New Year's Day.

CRAMOND

To the west of Edinburgh, Cramond is an attractive 18th-century village on the mouth of the River Almond, which flows over a weir in the centre of the village and into the Firth of Forth.

Dalmeny House **

Dalmeny House has been the seat of the **Earls of Rosebery** ever since the 17th century. Designed in 1815 in the Gothic style by William Wilkins (1778–1839), it houses a fine collection of **18th-century furniture** and **porcelain**, and also **portraits** by Raeburn, Reynolds and Gainsborough. Open July and August, Monday and Tuesday 12:00–17:30, Sunday 13:00–17:00.

South Queensferry

The 'Queen's Ferry' got its name from the saintly Queen Margaret, the Saxon English queen of King Malcolm III, who frequently crossed the Firth of Forth here while travelling between the royal palace at Dunfermline, in Fife, and Edinburgh. It sits in the shadow of two bridges – the colossal Forth Railway Bridge and the Forth Road Bridge.

THE FORTH BRIDGES

The Forth Rail Bridge was completed in 1890, carrying twin railway lines in a straight line for 3km (1.5 miles) across the Firth of Forth. Its three great cantilever spans reach 111m (364ft) above the high-water mark, mounted on gigantic caissons set into the bed of the firth. At the height of the Victorian era, this massive structure of girders and 4m (13ft) thick tubes was considered the eighth wonder of the world. When the **Forth Road Bridge** opened in 1964, it was the longest suspension bridge in the world, at 2km (1.25 miles), a record that has since been overtaken by several others. The main suspension towers are 157.5m (515ft) tall.

Below: *Rows of yachts at anchor on the River Almond at Cramond.*

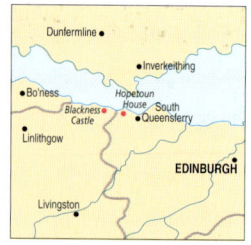

Below: *Linlithgow Palace,
now a ruin, was once Scotland's finest royal residence.*

Hopetoun House ***

Hopetoun House is one of the **grandest stately homes**
in Scotland. Set in some 40ha (100 acres) of woodland,
parkland and gardens, the house with its 170m (558ft)
colonnaded Corinthian frontage has been the seat of the
Earls of Hopetoun (later Marquesses of Linlithgow) since
1707. Within the house itself are superb drawing rooms
with **coloured silk walls**, set off by an elaborate Rococo
ceiling and some excellent **period paintings**, including a
gorgeous Canaletto of Venice. Hopetoun House is open
daily from 10 April to 27 September, 10:00–17:30.

Blackness Castle **

At Blackness village, this is a grim little stronghold.
Burned twice by the English in the 15th century, it was
rebuilt each time; during the French and Napoleonic Wars
it was an ammunition depot. Open daily 10:00–17:00,
closed Thursday afternoon and Friday October–March.

LINLITHGOW

The town of Linlithgow was a **royal seat** from the time of
David I, who built a fortified manor here in the 12th century, until the Union of the Crowns when King James VI
and I decamped to London, taking his court with him.

Linlithgow Heritage Trust Museum *

At 143 High Street the **Linlithgow Story** is told, with
exhibits on the ground floor stressing the town's royal
past, and the upper floor outlining the development of
Linlithgow's trade and industry.

Linlithgow Palace **

Linlithgow Palace stands just north of the High Street,
overlooking Linlithgow Loch. Now a ruined shell, in the
reign of James I it was the finest royal palace Scotland
had yet seen, and under James IV and V, Linlithgow was
the cradle of a Scottish Golden Age. It was destroyed by
fire in 1746, and with its empty windows gazing out over
the loch, it is one of Scotland's most **haunting** and
melancholy royal palaces. Open daily; hours vary.

Edinburgh at a Glance

BEST TIMES TO VISIT

It can be hard to find accommodation during the summer peak season (July–September), especially at the height of the Festival in August. In winter (November to mid-April) it can be very chilly in this region.

GETTING THERE

By air: Direct flights to Edinburgh from London and other major UK cities and from most European capitals. Edinburgh Airport Information, tel: (0131) 344 3111.
By road: The A68 and A7 highways lead to Edinburgh. For all public transport information, contact Traveline, 2 Cockburn Street, Edinburgh, tel: (0800) 232 323. Taxis operate from ranks at Waverley Station and Haymarket Station, and can be flagged down on the street or booked from Capital Castle Taxis, 2 Torphichen Street, Edinburgh, tel: (0131) 228 2555.

WHERE TO STAY

LUXURY
Channings, South Learmonth Gardens, Edinburgh EH4 1EX, tel: (0131) 315 2226, fax: (0131) 332 9631. Five Edwardian townhouses transformed into a stylish hotel with 48 rooms and terraced gardens.
Point Hotel, 34 Bread Street, Edinburgh EH3 9AF, tel: (0131) 221 5555, fax: (0131) 221 9929. Edinburgh's most

stylish hotel – decorated in vibrant colours, furnished with contemporary classics – has superior and executive rooms, and luxury jacuzzi suites.

MID-RANGE
Frederick House Hotel, 42 Frederick Street, Edinburgh EH2 1EX, tel: (0131) 226 1999, fax: (0131) 624 7064. Affordable, three-star comfort in the heart of the New Town.
Old Waverley Hotel, 43 Princes Street, Edinburgh EH2 2BY, tel: (0131) 556 4648, fax: (0131) 557 6316. Modern and comfortable, this 66-room hotel has views of the Castle.

BUDGET
Afton Town House Hotel, 6 Grosvenor Crescent, Edinburgh EH12 5EP, tel: (0131) 225 7033, fax: (0131) 225 7044. Affordable, central hotel close to Princes Street, in a Georgian-style building.

WHERE TO EAT

LUXURY
Martins Restaurant, 70 Rose Street North Lane, Edinburgh EH2 3DX, tel: (0131) 225 3106 (no fax). Small, discreet

and located in cobbled lane off Princes Street, this restaurant's menu stresses organic and wild foods.

MID-RANGE
EstEstEst, 135A George Street, Edinburgh, tel: (0131) 225 2555. Trendy, brasserie-style Italian restaurant on the fashionable George Street.
The Marque, 19 Causewayside, Edinburgh, tel: (0131) 466 6660. Opened in 1999, this is a fine nouvelle cuisine restaurant with a Scottish flavour.

BUDGET
City Café, 19 Blair Street, Edinburgh, tel: (0131) 220 0125. Trendy meeting place off the Royal Mile, affordable snacks and meals.
blue, 10 Cambridge Street, tel: (0131) 221 1222. This popular meeting place is on the first floor of the exciting Traverse Theatre.

USEFUL CONTACTS

Edinburgh and Lothians Tourist Board, 3 Princes Street, Edinburgh EH2 2QP, tel: (0131) 473 3800, fax: (0131) 473 3881.

EDINBURGH	J	F	M	A	M	J	J	A	S	O	N	D
AVERAGE TEMP. °C	6.2	6.4	8.5	11.2	14.2	17.1	18.4	18.2	16.3	13.3	9.1	7.1
AVERAGE TEMP. °F	43.2	43.5	47.3	52.2	57.6	62.8	65.1	64.8	61.3	56	48.4	44.8
HOURS OF SUN DAILY	2	3	5	6	8	8	8	7	5	4	3	2
RAINFALL mm	47	39	39	38	49	45	69	73	57	56	58	56
RAINFALL in	1.9	1.5	1.5	1.5	2	1.7	2.7	2.9	2.2	2.2	2.3	2.2

3
The Border Country

East of Edinburgh, the Firth of Forth widens as it meets the North Sea. This is a region of sweeping views out to sea, dramatic castles atop craggy headlands, and, inland, rolling farmland. South of Edinburgh, beyond the low range of the Pentland Hills, lies the rich farming country of Midlothian. Until the 1980s, the small towns of the region, including Lasswade, Bonnyrigg, Loanhead and Newtongrange, were coal-mining communities, but the Scottish coal industry is now virtually defunct. Beyond lie the rolling, treeless hills of the Borders, sheep-farming country with a rich, and often violent history of feuding, cattle stealing and border battles. The **River Tweed**, flowing eastward through the Borders to meet the North Sea at Berwick-upon-Tweed, forms the border with England for much of its length.

In Roman times, the region known as Valentia was a buffer zone between Hadrian's Wall and the heartland of Caledonia. The site of a Roman fort has been found at Eildon, near Melrose. Later, Scottish armies marched south through the Borders to victory or (more often) defeat, and English troops marched north to sack southern Scotland. For centuries, the Marches – as the lands either side of the Anglo-Scottish frontier are known – were notorious for the feuds and forays of their robber families.

Today – though its hills are still dotted with the ruined castles of the Border reivers – this is a gentler land of open sheep pastures and cheerful small market towns, and its inhabitants' aggressive instincts have been channelled into a passion for rugby.

DON'T MISS

*** Tantallon Castle: brooding ruin dramatically located on a high sea cliff.
*** Melrose Abbey: fine medieval abbey in the centre of a typical Borders town.
*** Abbotsford House: the mansion of one of Scotland's most famous writers, Sir Walter Scott.
*** Vikingar!: go back in time to the heroic heyday of the Lords of the Isles.
** Jedburgh Abbey: a ruined monastery with elaborate Norman architectural features.

Opposite: *The Borders castles are a reminder of the region's turbulent past.*

NORTH BERWICK AND KELSO

The small port of North Berwick stands near the mouth of the Firth of Forth, with fine North Sea views. Inland, Kelso was one of the most important Border towns during the Middle Ages, with a large abbey and a strategic castle.

Tantallon Castle ***

Tantallon, a colossal **ruin** on its beetling sea cliff 4km (2.5 miles) east of North Berwick, is surrounded on three sides by sea cliffs, defended on its landward side by deep ditches, and has a 16m (50ft) curtain wall up to 4m (12ft) thick. Open daily; hours vary.

CLUMSY COURTSHIP

In the 16th century Henry VIII thought to unite England and Scotland by marrying his son to the infant Mary, Queen of Scots. Thwarted by the Scottish nobles who supported a union with France, Henry sent the Earl of Hertford to ravage Scotland, burning Edinburgh in 1544 and initiating a reign of terror in southern Scotland. This 'rough wooing' ended only when a French army arrived in 1548 and spirited the young queen off to France.

Bass Rock ***

Visible from the harbour at North Berwick, about 1km (0.5 mile) offshore, is the Bass Rock, a 108m (350ft) volcanic core. The island, uninhabited except for huge numbers of **seabirds**, including guillemots, fulmars, razorbills, puffins, gulls and especially gannets, is reached by boat from the harbour. The Scottish Seabird Centre on the harbour is now the main attraction of North Berwick.

Floors Castle **

Still home of the local gentry, the Roxburghe dynasty, Floors Castle, some 1.6km (1 mile) northwest of Kelso, stands in beautiful gardens on the Tweed River, and houses some fine French antique furniture, paintings and tapestries. Open April–September; days and times vary.

JEDBURGH

One of the most important Scottish border strongholds of the 14th and 15th centuries, Jedburgh was guarded by a castle which was destroyed in 1409. Its large abbey, which was badly damaged in the border wars, was closed after the Reformation.

Jedburgh Abbey **

The most attractive part of this great ruin is the former abbey church, which became the parish kirk after the Reformation. It has elaborate Norman carvings, a noted rose window, and a 12th-century choir. The church is open daily; opening hours vary.

Mary, Queen of Scots House **

On Queen Street, this 16th-century house is said to have sheltered the ill-fated Queen in 1566, and houses a visitor centre which highlights her life and times. Open Easter to November, 10:00–17:00.

Ferniehurst Castle **

About 3km (2 miles) south of Jedburgh, this dinky 16th-century stronghold was the seat of the Kerr family, and is still owned by the Chief of the Kerrs, the Marquess of Lothian. Recently restored, it houses an information centre on the history of the Borders.

MELROSE AND GALASHIELS

On the banks of the Tweed, Melrose is one of the prettiest border towns. It was a garrison town in Roman times, but its top attraction is its ruined abbey. Galashiels has been a centre of the Borders woollen spinning and weaving industry since the 17th century.

BORDERS HISTORIC ROUTE

Starting south of the border at Carlisle, this 152km (95-mile) route rolls through the hills and dales of the border country, little visited and dotted with attractive border towns, evocative ruined castles, historic houses and fishing rivers, to end eventually in Edinburgh, Scotland's capital city.

Opposite: *Gannets soar above the Bass Rock lighthouse, where the Firth of Forth broadens into the North Sea.*
Below: *Ruined Tantallon Castle looks out to sea with the distinctive Bass Rock on the horizon.*

Above: *Dryburgh Abbey, sacked by English troops in the 16th century.*

Melrose Abbey ***

In the centre of town, Melrose Abbey was founded by the Cistercian order in 1136 and rebuilt in the 14th century. Much of its fine stonework, including parts of the nave and choir, survive. There is also a small museum. Open daily; opening hours vary.

Trimontium Exhibition **

In the Ormniston Institute, opposite the Abbey on the Square, this is a fascinating exhibition with models, plans and relics from the legionary fortress at Trimontium, a 150ha (370-acre) fort in the Eildon Hills, above Melrose. It is open from April to October, daily 10:30–16:30.

Dryburgh Abbey **

About 9km (6 miles) southeast of Melrose on the A68, Dryburgh was founded at the same time as Melrose. The cloister has survived, but only the transept survives of the main church. Open daily; hours vary.

Abbotsford House ***

Roughly 5km (3 miles) southeast of Galashiels on the A7, this was the mansion of **Sir Walter Scott**, who built it in 1822. It is packed with mementoes, and an armoury of historic weapons including Rob Roy's broadsword and Viscount Dundee's dragoon pistol. Open daily from mid-March to October; opening hours vary.

SELKIRK AND PEEBLES

Home of the **tweed-making trade**, Selkirk has strong associations with Sir Walter Scott, who was Sheriff (chief magistrate) of the county. Peebles, on the north bank of the Tweed, is the gateway to the Borders.

Sir Walter Scott's Courtroom **

In Market Place in the centre of Selkirk, this is the court-room where Sir Walter Scott judged local cases for some 30 years. Exhibits include his bench and chair, and portraits of Scott, Burns, and the Selkirk-born explorer **Mungo Park**. Open April–October, daily 10:30–16:30.

Neidpath Castle **

Just west of Peebles, Neidpath is a medieval tower house, typical of the architecture of the Borders at the time. Open Easter to September daily; hours vary.

Traquair House ***

Dating from the 12th century, Traquair is the oldest con-tinually inhabited house in Scotland. The home of a Jacobite family, its main gates were closed in 1745, pledged not to open again until there was a Stuart once again on the throne. They have remained closed, and a new drive gives access to the house and its collection of royal relics. Open May–September daily; hours vary.

DUMFRIES AND GALLOWAY

North of the Solway Firth, the Scottish mainland bulges westward into the Irish Sea. This region of southwest Scotland is **rich farming country** with a traditional rural character all of its own, and is strongly associated with the ploughman turned poet, **Robert Burns**.

Below left: *Selkirk's hills inspired Sir Walter Scott – the town's magistrate for 30 years – to write many of his historical romances.*

THE SHERIFF OF SELKIRK

Son of an Edinburgh lawyer, Sir Walter Scott (1771–1832) was born and educated in Edinburgh and trained as a barrister. He is vastly more famous as an author, and was hugely influential in creating a romantic, tartan-tinged myth of Scotland that survives to this day and is the powerhouse of the Scottish tourism industry, which owes Scott a great debt. Best known for works such as ***Rob Roy***, in which he turned an outlawed brigand and cattle-thief into a romantic hero (filmed in 1990 starring Liam Neeson); ***Waverley*** (which gave its name to Edinburgh's main station, in honour of the author, and to a brand of pen supposedly endorsed by him); ***Heart of Midlothian*** (which gave its name to one of Edinburgh's two football teams, Hearts); ***Ivanhoe***, and ***Hereward the Wake***.

Right: *Woodland and riverside, such as the view pictured here, are typical Borders scenery.*
Opposite: *Gretna Green's famous Old Blacksmith's Shop, scene of many a runaway wedding.*

Gretna Green *

On the Scottish border, 16km (10 miles) north of Carlisle on the A74, this village has a romantic reputation and is still a popular **wedding venue** but is otherwise undistinguished. In Gretna's heyday, when English marriage laws allowed a woman to marry only with her father's permission, runaway couples eloped to Gretna, the first settlement on the Scottish side of the border, where parental permission was not required, and were married in the **Old Blacksmith's Shop** (now a museum) with the smith's anvil as an altar.

Dumfries *

Dumfries, on the River Nith, is a farming centre and market town with a thriving Burns industry. The poet is buried in **St Michael's Churchyard**, in the town centre, where his remains were reinterred in a florid tomb in 1815. On Burns Street is **Burns House**, where he lived for the last three years of his life. An unremarkable 18th-century building, it houses his manuscripts and books.

Caerlaverock Castle ***

This unusual ruined castle constructed on a triangular plan was built by the Maxwells, a powerful Borders family, in 1270. Fine stone carvings survive, as do massive walls and towers. Open daily; opening hours vary.

RAIDERS' ROAD

Lowland Galloway is cattle-farming country, but much of the Galloway upland is rugged and forested, with more than 320km (200 miles) of way-marked walking and cycling trails. You can get off the beaten track the lazy way (by car) on the Raiders' Road: a former cattle drovers' trail, now a forestry track, which connects the A712 with the A762, running through pine woods with plenty of picnic spots beside lochs and rivers.

AYRSHIRE

Southwest of Glasgow and the Clyde, Ayrshire is farming country, but is placed firmly on the Scottish tourism map by the memory of **Robert Burns** (1759–96) who was born at Alloway, just south of the county town of Ayr.

Culzean Castle and Country Park ★★★

At the village of **Maybole** 19km (12 miles) south of Ayr, Culzean is a triumph of 18th-century aristocratic design, built between 1772 and 1792 to the plan of the architect Robert Adam for David, tenth Earl of Cassillis, on a cliff overlooking the sea. Surrounding the castle is Scotland's oldest **country park**, with deer, swans and forest walks. The castle is open April–October, daily 10:30–17:30, and the park is open year-round, daily 09:00 to sunset.

Alloway ★★★

This quiet farming town, 3km (2 miles) south of Ayr, is the birthplace of one of Scotland's best known men. The country's most famous bard was born in **Burns Cottage** in 1759 and lived here until the age of seven. Now a museum, it houses original manuscripts of Burns's songs and poems. Adjoining it is the **Burns Monument**, in mock-Classical style, built in 1823 and containing more relics of Burns. Open daily from April to October; hours vary.

Kirkoswald ★★★

This south Ayrshire village, on the A77 approximately 16km (10 miles) southwest of Alloway, has very strong Burnsian connections. The 18th-century Souter Johnnie's Cottage was the home of John Davidson, a village shoemaker and friend of Burns whom the poet used as the model for Souter Johnnie, Tam O' Shanter's 'honest, drouthy crony' in the famous poem. The cottage is open daily from Easter to October.

Mauchline **

Approximately 16km (11 miles) to the northeast of Ayr at the A76/B743 junction, this small town has a 15th-century castle and is best known for its typically Scottish decorated wooden box-ware (called 'Mauchline ware') and its connection with Robert Burns. The **Burns House Museum** on Castle Street was

Above: *Robert Burns was born in this modest cottage, now a museum.*
Below: *This Galloway farmer and his grandson are enjoying a ride.*

rented by Burns for his fiancée Jean Armour in 1788. The upper floor of this 18th-century house is furnished in contemporary style and occupied by talking models of the poet and his sweetheart. The museum also has a fine collection of Burnsiana and Mauchline ware. Open daily from Easter to October; hours vary.

Irvine **

This Ayrshire coastal town is well worth visiting for the **Scottish Maritime Museum** and Seaborn City in the harbour. It features traditional vessels, including a 'puffer' (one of the steamships that were the lifeline of many west coast communities in the 19th and early 20th centuries), a lifeboat and a harbour tug. Seaborn City, the latest addition, illustrates Glasgow's history as an Atlantic seaport. It is open year-round; times and days vary.

Largs ***

Inspired by the decisive battle between the Scots and Norwegians in 1263, **Vikingar!** is a **multimedia centre** which takes you back in time to the heroic heyday of the unique Celtic-Norse culture of the Lords of the Isles. Open year-round; days and times vary.

The Border Country at a Glance

BEST TIMES TO VISIT

The Borders are best visited between April and October, as many attractions are closed during the winter.

GETTING THERE

By air: Direct flights to Edinburgh from London and other major UK cities and from most European capitals. Edinburgh Airport Information, tel: (0131) 344 3111. There are also direct flights to Glasgow International Airport, about 30 minutes from the city centre, tel: (0141) 887 1111. Some airlines also use Prestwick Airport, about 45 miles southwest of Glasgow, tel: (01292) 479 822.

By road: Regional buses run from Edinburgh's St Andrew Square bus station, tel: (0131) 313 1515, to all the border towns and Scottish cities.

By rail: For rail information, contact ScotRail, tel: (0141) 335 4260, or Virgin Trains, tel: (0131) 559 1007.

GETTING AROUND

By rail: Services operate to all points in Strathclyde, southern and central Scotland from Glasgow's Queen Street and Central stations. Contact Strathclyde Passenger Transport, tel: (0141) 332 7133, for timetables and routes.

By road: The A8/A78 runs along the south side of the Firth of Clyde and the Ayrshire coast. Buses operate throughout the region from Glasgow.

Scottish Citylink Coaches, Buchanan Bus Station, Glasgow, tel: (08705) 505 050.

WHERE TO STAY

LUXURY

Cringeltie House Hotel, Peebles EH45 8PL, tel: (01721) 730 233, fax: (01721) 730 244. Traditional Borders manor in huge garden, built in 1861. Romantic, with a restaurant.

Peebles Hotel Hydro, Peebles EH45 8LX, tel: (01721) 720 602, fax: (01721) 722 999. Spa-style hotel built in 1907.

The Eisenhower Apartment, Culzean Castle, Maybole, Ayrshire KA19 8LE, tel: (01655) 884 455, fax: (01655), 884 503. A splendidly decorated National Trust property with magnificent views and a fine restaurant.

MID-RANGE

The Open Arms, Dirleton EH39 5EG, tel: (01620) 850 241, fax: (01620) 850 570. Family-owned hotel in village centre with view of castle.

BUDGET

Low Kirkbride Farmhouse, Auldgirth, Dumfries DG2 0SP, tel/fax: (01387) 820 258. Family-run bed and breakfast on a working farm.

WHERE TO EAT

LUXURY

Selkirk Arms Hotel, High Street, Kircudbright DG6 4JG, tel: (01557) 330 402, fax: (01557) 331 639. A superb gourmet restaurant in a small mid-range hotel in the centre.

MID-RANGE

Craigadam, Castle Douglas, Kircudbrightshire DG7 3HU, tel/fax: (01556) 650 233. Elegant farmhouse with fine home cooking.

Auld Alliance, Castle Street, Kirkcudbright DG6 4JA, tel: (01577) 330 569. Excellent cooking blending Scottish produce with French influences.

BUDGET

Simply Scottish, High Street, Jedburgh TD8 6AG, tel: (01835) 864 696. Attractive modern bistro in centre of Jedburgh with local produce.

Cobbles Inn Restaurant, 7 Bowmont Street, Kelso, tel: (01573) 223 548. Traditional inn-style atmosphere in an attractive, black and white listed building dating from the 1800s. Good pub meals.

USEFUL CONTACTS

Scottish Borders Tourist Board, Murray's Green, Jedburgh TD8 6BE, tel: (01835) 863 435, fax: (01835) 864 099.

Ayrshire and Arran Tourist Board, Burns House, Burns Statue Square, Ayr KA7 1UP, tel: (01292) 288 688, fax: (01292) 288 686.

Dumfries and Galloway Tourist Board, 64 Whitesands, Dumfries DG1 2RS, tel: (01387) 253 862, fax: (01387) 245 556.

4
Glasgow

With a population of almost one million, Glasgow is Scotland's **largest city** and is keenly aware of its rivalry with Edinburgh. Less than 80km (50 miles) separate the two, yet the psychological gulf between east and west coast seems much wider. If Edinburgh cultivates an image of well-bred, cultured gentility, Glasgow sometimes seems to revel in its reputation as tough, egalitarian and brash. Yet Glasgow has a strong cultural tradition too, one which came to the fore in the 1990s, and which has been carefully cultivated.

Though its name derives from the Gaelic *glas ghu* – which means 'the dear, green place' – the sprawling cityscape on either side of the River Clyde could hardly be further from the picture the name evokes. The outer suburbs hold very little of interest for the visitor, but central Glasgow is one of Britain's liveliest cities, with some magnificent art galleries and fascinating museums, sophisticated shopping, great places to eat and drink, and rocking nightlife. Home of **Scottish Royal Ballet**, **Scottish Opera**, and the **Glasgow School of Art**, the city can also claim to be the hub of Scotland's active film and television scene.

Glasgow's first fortunes were made in importing tobacco and cotton from Britain's new colonies in America. With the Industrial Revolution, the city became one of the **great industrial centres** of the British Empire, and Clydeside became synonymous with shipbuilding. Glasgow's most striking architecture and cultural exhibits date from this Victorian zenith.

DON'T MISS

*** Burrell Collection: eclectic, esoteric and exotic.
*** People's Palace: a monument to Glasgow's working-class history.
** Hunterian Art Gallery: the world's best collection of the works of Charles Rennie Mackintosh.
** Glasgow Cathedral: the best preserved of Scotland's Gothic churches.
** Barras Market: century-old covered market with countless interesting stalls.

Opposite: *Glasgow blooms in spring – the city is well named 'the dear, green place'.*

Above: *Statues of 19th-century achievers line Glasgow's George Square.*

CENTRAL GLASGOW

Most of Glasgow's attractions, restaurants and **nightlife** are north of the River Clyde, with Anderston Quay, the Broomielaw, and Clyde Street running along the river. **George Square** is a handy starting point for exploring.

City Chambers *

The city council meets in this mock-Italian **Renaissance building** on the east of George Square. Inside are sweeping marble staircases and an impressive banqueting hall.

The Lighthouse *

At 11 Mitchell Lane, this building houses a **Charles Rennie Mackintosh Interpretation Centre**, temporary exhibitions, and a rooftop viewing platform. Open daily, 09:00–17:30.

Collins Gallery *

On the **University of Strathclyde** campus off George Street, this very lively **contemporary** gallery operates changing exhibitions, from photography to modern painting and sculpture. Open from Monday to Friday, 10:00–17:00.

People's Palace, Glasgow Green **

Glasgow Green, 52ha (129 acres) beside the Clyde, is the city's **oldest park**. The People's Palace, opened in 1898, is a **monument** to workers and industries of Glasgow, with collections relating to the tobacco trade and crafts such as ceramics and stained glass, as well as working-class political and social movements. Open Monday to Saturday, 10:00–17:00.

Barras Market **

The Barras, a century-old **covered market** approximately 500m (550yd) east of Glasgow Cross, is a wonderful place to hunt for **bargains** of all kinds, with an amazing assortment of more than 800 stalls and shops selling everything imaginable, from antiques to ants' eggs. Closed Monday–Tuesday.

Tenement House **

This building at 145 Buccleuch Street dates from 1892 and has been preserved as a **museum of urban life** and **domestic architecture** of the late 19th century. Original features include the kitchen range, sink, coal bunker and built-in box beds typical of the time. Open from March to November; days and times vary.

Glasgow Cathedral **

The cathedral of St Mungo, one of the earliest Celtic saints, is the best preserved of Scotland's great Gothic churches. The mid-13th-century crypt is its most striking feature. Open daily; hours vary.

Glasgow School of Art **

Located at 167 Renfrew Street, the college is one of the largest British art schools, noted for fine art, craft and design. The School of Art is housed in the Mackintosh Building, designed by one of its most famous alumni, **Charles Rennie Mackintosh**. It is open from Monday to Friday, 09:30–17:00.

WEST OF THE CENTRE

The M8 motorway, curving from the east to cross the River Clyde by the Kingston Bridge, forms the perimeter of the city centre. Sauchiehall Street leads westward from the centre to Kelvingrove Park, the Glasgow University campus, and some of the city's important museums and galleries.

BY DESIGN

Born in Glasgow in 1868, **Charles Rennie Mackintosh** was one of Scotland's best known designers and architects, creating a distinctive decorative style which is much imitated still. Buildings designed by him, including the **Glasgow School of Art** and the **Willow Tea Room**, are among the most attractive in Glasgow, and the **Hill House** in Helensburgh is one of his finest commissions for a private client. Furniture and decorative objects designed by Mackintosh can be found in several museums and exhibitions in Edinburgh and Glasgow. Mackintosh died in 1928.

Below: *The Willow Tea Room, designed by Glasgow style guru Charles Rennie Mackintosh.*

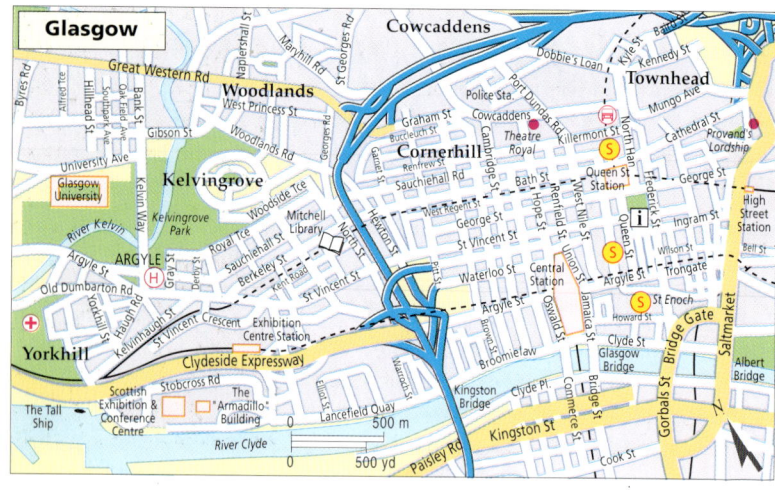

Queen's Cross Church *

Situated at 870 Garscube Road, to the west of the city centre, this church was designed by Charles Rennie Mackintosh. Built between 1897 and 1899, it houses the **Charles Rennie Mackintosh Society** and its exhibition. It is open on Tuesday, Thursday and Friday 12:00–17:30, as well as Sunday afternoon.

The Tall Ship at Glasgow Harbour **

Moored opposite 100 Stobcross Road on the north bank of the Clyde, the 19th-century sailing vessel *Glenlee*, built in 1896, is one of the last tall ships to be built on the Clyde. Open daily, 10:00 to dusk.

Glasgow Science Centre

Opposite the Tall Ship on the south bank of the Clyde, Scotland's newest attraction will open at Easter 2001, housing a 120-seat planetarium and interactive displays on cutting-edge scientific advances in the 21st century.

Opposite: *The interior of Kibble Palace at Glasgow's Botanic Gardens shelters rare tropical orchids, ferns and begonias.*
Below: *Glasgow School of Art, designed by Charles Rennie Mackintosh.*

Museum of Transport *

Housed in the grand 19th-century Kelvin Hall at 1 Bunhouse Road, this newish museum's most interesting feature is its mock-up of a typical Glasgow street in 1938, with trams and horse-drawn carts. More Glasgow trams and buses, vans and lorries, steam engines and cars from the 1930s to the present round out the collection. Open daily; hours vary.

Kelvingrove Park **

Landscaped by the famous Victorian landscape architect Sir Joseph Paxton in 1852, the 34ha (84-acre) park, with Glasgow University on its north side and the Kelvingrove Art Galleries to the south, is Glasgow's largest sector of urban greenery.

Kelvingrove Art Gallery and Museum **

On the south side of the park, Glasgow's city art gallery has a special collection of **French Impressionists** and **post-Impressionists**, some old masters, and furniture by Charles Rennie Mackintosh. Open daily; hours vary.

Hunterian Museum and Art Gallery ***

The Hunterian Museum is Scotland's oldest, dating from 1807 and gifted to the city by William Hunter with a collection of archaeological relics, coins and material relating to the history of Glasgow University. Much more gripping is the attached **Hunterian Art Gallery**, with the world's best collection of the work of Charles Rennie Mackintosh and a fine collection of **Scottish paintings**. Both are housed within the **University of Glasgow** buildings at Hillhead Street, 3km (2 miles) west of the city centre. Open Monday–Saturday, 09:30–17:00.

Botanic Gardens **

North of the University, at 730 Great Western Road, the Botanic Gardens' famous **Kibble Palace** glasshouses shelter rare tropical orchids, tree ferns and an outstanding collection of begonias. Entered from Great Western Road, the gardens are open daily; hours vary.

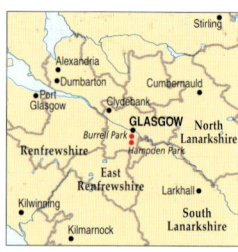

SOUTH OF THE CLYDE

The fantastically eclectic **Burrell Collection** is the main reason for crossing the river, but in the same area the **Pollok House** and **The House for an Art Lover** are also worth seeing, while the Scottish National Stadium at Hampden Park is a place of pilgrimage for followers of football history in the making.

The Burrell Collection ***

The Burrell Collection, located in **Pollok Country Park** some 4km (3 miles) south of the city centre, could be the single most interesting attraction in Glasgow. Donated to the city by Sir William and Lady Burrell, the collection ranges from *objets d'art* and works by 19th-century French artists to gorgeous textiles, fine ceramics, antique furnishings and stained glass. Open daily; hours vary.

Pollok House *

On the opposite side of **Pollok Country Park** from the Burrell Collection stands this gracious 18th-century manor. Within is the **Stirling Maxwell** collection of European paintings, as well as 18th-century silver, glass and furniture. Open daily; hours vary.

House for an Art Lover **

Designed by Charles Rennie Mackintosh in 1901, this unique building in Bellahouston Park (the entrance is at 10 Dumbreck Road) was built in 1996 and its suites of rooms reflect **Mackintosh's genius** for every aspect of interior design. Open from April to September, Sunday–Friday 10:00–16:00; October–March opening hours vary; tel: (0141) 353 4449 for details.

Hampden, Scotland's National Stadium **

The Stadium at **Hampden Park**, some 8km (5 miles) south of the city centre, is a shrine to the game that is Scotland's national obsession and also houses the **Scottish Museum of Football**. The museum, opened in January 2000, celebrates Scotland's footballing history and its greatest players. Open daily.

Glasgow at a Glance

BEST TIMES TO VISIT

Glasgow can be visited year-round, but is most popular during the summer months, while accommodation in the rest of the region can be hard to find in the mid-June to end-August summer high season and from October to April, when some guesthouses and hotels are closed.

GETTING THERE

By air: Direct flights from North America, Europe, London and other UK cities to Glasgow International Airport, about 30 minutes from the city centre, tel: (0141) 887 1111. Some flights also use Prestwick Airport, about 72km (45 miles) southwest of Glasgow, tel: (01292) 479 822.

By rail: Trains from London via Manchester and Carlisle take around 5 hours 30 minutes and arrive at Glasgow Central Station. Edinburgh trains arrive and leave from Glasgow Queen Street, as do trains to Stirling, Perth, Dundee, Aberdeen and Inverness. Trains also run from Queen Street via Dumbarton to Oban, Fort William and Mallaig. Rail information: ScotRail, tel: (0141) 335 4260; Virgin Trains, tel: (0131) 559 1007.

By road: Express coach services operate to London on the main motorway from Buchanan Street Coach Station, Glasgow. Contact Scottish Citylink Coaches, tel: (08705) 505 050.

By sea: Ferries to Ballycastle in Northern Ireland leave from Troon.

GETTING AROUND

Glasgow has a single-line underground system which loops around the city centre, stopping at Buchanan Street (with a travelator link to Queen Street rail station) but not at Central Station. Outer suburbs are connected by an efficient suburban overground train service and bus services. Contact Strathclyde Passenger Transport, tel: (0141) 332 7133. Taxis are metered cabs and can be flagged down on the street, with cab ranks at both main stations.

WHERE TO STAY

LUXURY
The Devonshire Hotel, 5 Devonshire Gardens, Glasgow G12 0UX, tel: (0141) 339 7878, fax: (0141) 339 3980. Voted one of Scotland's most romantic hotels.

MID-RANGE
Ewington Hotel, Balmoral Terrace, 132 Queens Drive, Glasgow G42 8QW, tel: (0141) 432 1152, fax: (0141) 422 2030. Comfortable hotel on a Victorian terrace, six minutes by rail from city centre.

BUDGET
Babbity Bowster, 16–18 Blackfriars Street, Glasgow G1 1PE, tel: (0141) 552 5055, fax: (0141) 552 7774. Lively

inn in Merchant City district, comfortable rooms, Scottish cooking, live music and bar.

WHERE TO EAT

LUXURY
Lux, Great Western Road, Glasgow G12 0XP, tel: (0141) 576 7576. One of Glasgow's top restaurants serving Scottish produce with an imaginative new style.
The Ubiquitous Chip, 12 Ashton Lane, Glasgow G12 8SJ, tel: (0141) 334 5007. One of Glasgow's best loved restaurants (established 1971) with a menu blending Scottish and international influences.

MID-RANGE
Stravaigin, 28 Gibson Street, Hillhead, Glasgow G12 BNX, tel: (0141) 334 2665. Popular brasserie-style restaurant.
The Brasserie, 176 West Regent Street, Glasgow G2 4RL, tel: (0141) 248 3801. Elegant brasserie, popular for business lunches, central.

BUDGET
Bouzy Rouge, 111 West Regent Street, Glasgow G2 2RU, tel: (0141) 221 8804. Centrally located bar-restaurant, Scottish food with an international flavour.

USEFUL CONTACTS

Greater Glasgow and Clyde Valley Tourist Board, 11 George Square, Glasgow G2 1DY, tel: (0141) 204 4400, fax: (0141) 221 3524.

5
Central Scotland

Central Scotland is a region that is full of surprises, straddling the country from the moors and glens of the Trossachs to the shores of Loch Lomond, the Firth of Forth and the coasts of Fife. It is a region steeped in history, where many of the bloodiest battles in Scotland's history were fought, and where many of its kings and queens lived and died.

On the Atlantic coast, the **Mull of Kintyre** dangles from the body of the mainland, sheltering Arran and the Firth from the open Atlantic Ocean. Loch Fyne, a long, narrow arm of the sea which stretches northwards from the Firth of Clyde, cuts off the Mull of Kintyre from mainland Argyll. The fishing and ferry port of Oban, close to the mouth of the Great Glen, is the gateway to the southern Hebridean islands of Jura, Islay, Colonsay, Mull, Coll and Tiree.

Towns such as Stirling are rich in centuries-old castles, colleges and cathedrals, while the hills of central Scotland and the cliffs and bays of the North Sea coast conceal some of the most attractive farming and fishing villages in Scotland.

Fife, jutting into the North Sea between the Firths of Tay and Forth, has been described as 'a beggar's mantle [cloak] fringed with gold', a description that referred to the contrast between the sandy beaches of its east coast and the grimy pitheads and slagheaps of its coal-mining hinterland. The fishing villages of the east coast are delightful, and historic towns such as Dunfermline and St Andrews are well worth a visit.

DON'T MISS

*** Inveraray Castle: the seat of Scotland's most powerful clan chief.
*** Stirling Castle: this is one of Scotland's most important fortresses.
*** Falkland Palace: one of the country's best preserved medieval royal palaces.
** Arran: beautiful island landscapes near Glasgow.
** St Andrews Cathedral: evocative ruin of one of Scotland's great churches.
** Dunfermline Abbey: a Norman church with an ancient royal history.

Opposite: *The Trossachs offer lovely scenery close to Scotland's biggest cities.*

Below: *Arran, with its hills and beaches, is the most accessible of the Scottish isles.*

ARGYLL

One of Scotland's most beautiful scenic regions, Argyll is divided by sea lochs into a collection of narrow peninsulas. In the middle of the Firth of Forth, Arran and Bute are the most accessible of Scottish islands. They were very popular, affordable holiday destinations for generations of Glaswegians.

Arran **

Arran has sandy beaches and good hill-walking. A single main road, the A841, encircles the island, which has only two villages – **Brodick**, the larger, on the east coast and **Lochranza**, close to Arran's northern tip.

The small port of Brodick is the gateway to Arran. At Anchor Hotel Park, Comrie Road, the small, independent **Arran and Argyll Transport Museum** features photographs and paraphernalia from the old-time paddlesteamers, trains and buses. The town's **castle** is Brodick's main attraction. The oldest part is a 13th-century tower, but the most impressive part of the building is the lavish early Victorian mansion wing. Within are lavishly decorated rooms and a fine collection of porcelain, paintings and silverware.

Goatfell, the island's highest peak, at 874m (2866ft), and the neighbouring **Cir Mhor** at 798m (2618ft) offer superb views of the island and the Firth of Clyde, as well as rock-climbing and ridge-walking.

Central Scotland

Bute **

Bute is somewhat less impressive than Arran, and its main appeal lies in its easy access from Glasgow. The major attraction of the small ferry port of **Rothesay** is the award-winning **Mount Stuart House** and **Gardens**, a stunning 18th- to 19th-century baronial manor set amid some 120ha (300 acres) of woodland and gardens. On Stuart Street in the centre of Rothesay, the **Bute Museum** contains exhibits from the island, relating to its wildlife, geology and history.

Mull of Kintyre **

Immortalized by ex-Beatle **Paul McCartney**, who has made his home there, the Mull of Kintyre is a narrow peninsula situated well off the tourist track leading from Glasgow northwards to Loch Lomond, Glencoe and the Highlands. Relatively little visited, it has some beautiful scenery, while its little 'capital', **Campbeltown**, is a charming harbour town.

Oban *

Oban is an attractive small town in its own right, with a heritage redolent of both whisky distilling and herring fishing. Founded more than two centuries ago, the **Distillery**, situated at Stafford Street in the town centre, is renowned for its excellent malt whisky. Tours of the distillery show visitors how whisky is made, and there are tastings of the finished product.

Opposite bottom:
Goatfell, Arran's highest peak, offers superb views of the island and the Firth of Clyde.

CLAN CAMPBELL

The mountains and sea lochs of Argyll, in the shadow of Ben Cruachan, were the heartland of the Clan Campbell, whose clan chiefs sided early with the Crown, first in Edinburgh and then in London, against their ancestral enemies, Clan Donald, the Grigarach (MacGregors) and later the Stuarts of Appin. As the government's enforcers in the southern Highlands, they achieved great power, wealth and huge estates, which the Dukes of Argyll retain to this day. The regiment which they levied, the Argyll and Sutherland Highlanders, became one of the most prestigious of the elite kilted soldiery of the British Empire.

ARGYLL TOURIST ROUTE

Starting at Tarbet on the northern tip of Loch Lomond, this 238km (148-mile) route climbs through the hills to emerge on the shores of Loch Fyne, famous for its kippers, and Inveraray, seat of Clan Campbell and one of Scotland's finest castles. Then it runs north, to the lively port of Oban, with superb views across the Firth of Lorne to Mull and neighbouring islands. From Oban, the route travels through wild country to Ballachulish and Fort William, Ben Nevis, and the Great Glen.

Below: *Inveraray Castle, formidable ancestral seat of the Clan Campbell and the Dukes of Argyll.*

Loch Etive ***

The small town of **Taynuilt**, about 15km (9 miles) east of Oban on the A85, is the gateway to cruises through the stunning scenery of Loch Etive, an outstandingly beautiful sea loch. Long and narrow, it stretches some 32km (20 miles) from Connel Bridge, where it meets the sea, to the slopes of Glencoe. Inaccessible by road, it shelters grey and common seals, red deer, and golden eagle.

Inveraray ***

The town of Inveraray, on the north shore of Loch Fyne, is the ancestral seat of the Campbell Dukes of Argyll. The grim stone **Inveraray Jail** on Church Square recreates the conditions of a 19th-century prison around 1820, with uniformed guards, lifelike talking figures and a trial in progress in the former county courtroom. On The Avenue, the 40m (126ft) granite **Bell Tower** is Inveraray's unmissable landmark and houses the second heaviest peal of bells in the world.

Just 1km (0.5 mile) north of the town centre, the 18th-century **Inveraray Castle** was completed after the final defeat of the Jacobite clans at Culloden. The magnificent interior was designed by Robert Mylne for the fifth Duke, and a fine collection of portraits by Ramsay, Raeburn and Gainsborough hangs within.

Argyll Wildlife Park **

On the A83 at **Dalchenna**, 3km (2 miles) southwest of Inveraray, this 24ha (60-acre) park is mainly for the birds, with many rare owl species – including eagle owls – and one of Britain's finest wildfowl collections. Open daily; times vary.

LOCH LOMOND AND THE TROSSACHS

Glasgow's urban residential sprawl extends some 20km (13 miles) westward along the north bank of the Clyde and 10km (6 miles) north. Beyond the fringes of the city, there is a surprisingly abrupt transition to the open spaces, with the wooded 'bonnie banks and braes' of Loch Lomond, only 16km (10 miles) beyond the city limits, as a curtain-raiser for scenery which becomes ever more spectacular as you head north.

The Hill House ***
On Upper Colquhoun Street, in **Helensburgh**, 34km (21 miles) northwest of Glasgow, this is regarded as Charles Rennie Mackintosh's finest design for a **private home**. It was built in 1903–04 and is still a timeless classic. Open April–October, daily 13:30–17:30.

Argyll Forest Park **
This 24,281ha (60,000-acre) expanse of woodland off the A83, 8km (5 miles) northwest of **Arrochar** village (close to the northern extremity of Loch Lomond), offers magnificent forest walks.

Loch Lomond ***
Britain's **largest lake** is surrounded by wooded hills and dotted with islands. The small town of **Balloch**, at the southern end of the loch, is the main base for touring, cruising and staying on Loch Lomond. Two small, uninhabited islands, **Bucinch** and **Ceardach**, are the property of the National Trust for Scotland and are open year-round (there is no designated landing place).

Callander *
Callander is a farming town and the gateway to the rolling hill country of the **Trossachs**, an expanse of hills, moorland, lochs and forests that extends eastward from the shores of Loch Lomond.

The **Rob Roy and Trossachs Visitor Centre** on Ancaster Square in the town centre tells the much-romanticized story of Rob Roy MacGregor – who was turned into a romantic hero by Sir Walter Scott – amid the stunningly beautiful Highland scenery of the Trossachs, his stamping ground.

Above: *Loch Lomond, Britain's largest lake, is a veritable inland sea.*

ROB ROY

Generally known as Rob Roy (Red Robert) because of the colour of his hair, **Rob Roy MacGregor** (1671–1734) was a herdsman and Jacobite sympathizer who took to cattle rustling and thieving to feed his clan. Declared an **outlaw** by the Duke of Montrose, Rob plundered the duke's lands and re-peatedly escaped from prison, earning a reputation similar to England's Robin Hood. Pardoned in 1725, he spent his final years in peaceful retirement.

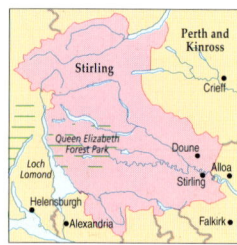

STIRLING AND AROUND

Built around a steep-sided crag crowned by a forbidding castle, Stirling looks a little like Edinburgh in miniature. It was a strategic **fortress** until the 18th century, and one of the most strongly fortified in Scotland. Among the town's sights are monuments to the two great heroes of the Wars of Independence.

Stirling Castle ***

On a 76m (250ft) crag, Stirling Castle dominates the town and was frequently a refuge for Scottish monarchs when Edinburgh was in hostile hands. Among its most striking aspects are the towers built by James IV, the fine Renaissance palace added by James V, and the 16th-century hall and royal chapel. The castle also houses the regimental museum of the Argyll and Sutherland Highlanders, Scotland's oldest kilted regiment.

Argyll's Lodging **

On Castle Wynd, opposite the entrance to the castle, this recently refurbished 17th-century building was the home of Sir William Alexander of Menstrie, who became Earl of Stirling. Open daily; opening hours vary.

Stirling Old Town Jail **

Opposite Argyll's Lodging, the grim cells of the town lock-up have been turned into a scary visitor attraction. It is open daily; opening hours vary.

SCOTTISH CASTLES

From Edinburgh on its crag to lonely ruins like Dunnottar, castles are **symbols of Scotland**. Because of Scotland's unsettled state, clan chiefs and Lowland lairds alike went on living in fortified homes long after the squires of more peaceful England had abandoned their feudal strongholds for more comfortable manor houses. Most Scottish castles which can be seen today date from the 16th and 17th centuries. Many more, like **Balmoral**, were built in the peaceful 19th century and incorporate features like 'pepper-pot' corner turrets, or bartizans, and square or round towers. Some of the most imposing structures, like **Edinburgh** and **Stirling**, continued as garrison fortresses long after the final pacification of Scotland in the18th century.

Menstrie Castle *

This small, fort-like castle was the birthplace of **Sir William Alexander of Menstrie**, founder of Nova Scotia. A small exhibition tells the story of his ill-fated attempt to set up a Scottish colony in Canada. Open Easter, May to September, Wednesday and Sunday afternoon.

Bannockburn Heritage Centre **

About 3km (2 miles) south of Stirling off the M9, the Heritage Centre tells the story of one of Scotland's few decisive victories. The **Battle of Bannockburn**, fought in 1314, took place about a mile further west. The centre is open from April to October, daily 10:00–18:00.

Doune **

Doune stands on the edge of the Highlands, about 13km (8 miles) northwest of Stirling off the M80. In medieval times it was a frontier town between the relatively civilized Lowlands and the clans of the north, who traded cattle here for manufactured goods such as the silver mounted 'Doune pistols' they favoured. Though a picturesque ruin, **Doune Castle** is one of Scotland's better preserved medieval strongholds.

Dollar Glen and Castle Campbell **

The village of **Dollar**, about 17km (11 miles) east of Stirling, is a convenient stop on the road to Fife. Just off the A91, 1.5km (1 mile) north of Dollar village, a lushly wooded glen, where waterfalls tumble through steep clefts, provides a lovely walk to **Castle Campbell**, a 15th-century stronghold of **Clan Campbell**. The castle is open daily; opening times vary.

DUNFERMLINE AND AROUND

A rather unassuming town close to the Forth coast, Dunfermline was one of Scotland's earliest capitals. Today, it is gradually becoming a residential annex of Edinburgh, 20 minutes away by rail.

Above: *The picturesque ruins of Castle Campbell, 15th-century stronghold of the clan.*
Opposite: *Stirling Castle for centuries held the key to control of Scotland.*

NATIONAL WALLACE MONUMENT

This grandiose 19th-century tower, 67m (220ft) high, stands atop Abbey Craig, 2km (1.5 miles) northeast of Stirling on the A907, and is clearly visible for miles around. From the top there are panoramic views of Stirling and the surrounding countryside. Open April–October daily; hours vary.

Above: *A view of the Lomond hills across Loch Leven, the largest loch in the Lowlands.*
Opposite: *Loch Leven, where Mary Queen of Scots was imprisoned in the island castle.*

THE MIDAS TOUCH

The epitome of the Scottish self-made man, **Andrew Carnegie** (1835–1919) was the son of a Dunfermline weaver. When his family emigrated to Pennsylvania he started work as a telegraph boy, and eventually became the iron and steel king of America – and the richest man in the world. Instead of keeping his US$400 million fortune, he retired from business in 1901 to distribute his wealth by founding libraries, parks and meeting halls throughout the world. When he died in 1919 he had given away US$350 million, but there is still plenty left – the **British Carnegie Trust** alone gives away US$150 a minute.

Dunfermline Abbey and Palace Visitor Centre **

The 11th-century Benedictine abbey is almost ruined, with only parts of its refectory walls still standing, but the church is intact, with a fine Norman nave. A heritage centre is housed in the attractively restored **Abbot House**, once the home of Benedictine abbots. Open daily; opening times vary.

Andrew Carnegie Birthplace Museum **

Located on Moodie Street, to the north of the Abbey, a small weaver's cottage was the birthplace of Andrew Carnegie, the great 19th-century **philanthropist**. The museum is open daily; opening times vary.

North Queensferry ***

North Queensferry, 8km (5 miles) south of Dunfermline, stands below the huge girders of the Forth Railway Bridge (*see* page 43). About 100m (110yd) from North Queensferry Harbour, the award-winning **Deep Sea World** is built into a flooded quarry with the world's longest underwater tunnel and many North Sea marine species to see.

Inchcolm Island and Abbey **

Founded in 1192 by Alexander I, the ruined Abbey stands on the tiny island of Inchcolm, in the middle of the Firth of Forth, which is reached by boat from North Queensferry. The island is **uninhabited** except for seals and seabirds. Open April–September, daily 09:30–18:30.

Kinross and Loch Leven *

The small manufacturing town of Kinross, midway between Dunfermline and Perth, stands on the shores of wide Loch Leven, where Mary, Queen of Scots was imprisoned in 1567 in **Loch Leven Castle**, a grim square tower standing on an island in the loch. Access to the castle is by boat from Kinross; open daily from April to September; opening hours vary.

Kirkcaldy *

Kirkcaldy, on the North Sea, is known as the birthplace of **Robinson Crusoe** and also of Adam Smith, the father of free market economics. In the **War Memorial Gardens** in the centre of town, **Kirkcaldy Museum and Art Gallery** has a fine collection by Scottish painters of the 19th and 20th centuries, and a lively local history exhibition.

Falkland Palace ***

Roughly 17km (11 miles) north of Kirkcaldy, at Falkland village, the Royal Palace of Falkland was the hunting lodge and country home of eight Stuart monarchs. Completed in 1541, it is Scotland's finest example of Renaissance architecture, with a beautiful **Chapel Royal**. Open daily April–October; opening times vary.

Cupar **

A small town in the Fife area, located in the middle of farming country, Cupar is well worth a stop for its main tourist attraction, a fine early 20th-century mansion. The **Hill of Tarvit Mansion House** was built for a Dundee jute millionaire, F B Sharp, and it houses a superb collection of French, antique Scottish and Chippendale furniture, as well as artwork and Chinese porcelain.

Fife Folk Museum **

On the B939 at Ceres, 9 km (6 miles) southeast of Cupar, a cluster of traditional buildings houses a collection of furniture, tools, utensils and clothes, showcasing the daily lives of people in rural Fife a century and more ago. Open April–October, daily 14:00–19:00.

THE NEUK OF FIFE

The coast south of Fife Ness, the easternmost headland of Fife, is known as the Neuk (corner) of Fife and shelters a string of attractive fishing villages, connected by a walking trail known as the Fife Coastal Path.

A TRAGIC QUEEN

Mary, Queen of Scots, was unlucky even by Stuart standards. Her first husband, the French King Francois II, died after only 17 months on the throne. Back in Scotland, she married her cousin, Lord Darnley, who was soon murdered, perhaps by the Earl of Bothwell, Scotland's Lord High Admiral. He became her third husband only eight weeks later. Scandalized, the powerful Protestant Lords forced Mary to abdicate, crowned her baby son (the issue of her second marriage) as King James VI, and imprisoned her in Loch Leven Castle. Escaping, she raised an army but was defeated at Langside by the Protestant Regent, her half-brother, the Earl of Moray. In 1568, she fled to England, where her cousin Elizabeth I imprisoned her for 19 years, then had her executed.

Pittenweem **

This fishing village is the southernmost of the Neuk of
Fife. About 4km (3 miles) northwest of Pittenweem,
Kellie Castle is one of Lowland Scotland's oldest and finest
castles. Completed in 1606, its oldest parts are 250 years
older. Within, the superb panelling, plasterwork and
furniture are the work of Scottish architect, **Sir Robert
Lorimer**, who restored the castle in the late 19th century.

Anstruther **

Fishing is still a way of life in Anstruther, 8km (5 miles)
east of Pittenweem, with a modern fishing fleet in its harbour. Older wooden vessels and fishing gear have been
relegated to a museum, the **Scottish Fisheries Museum**.

Crail *

Crail, located approximately 7km (4 miles) northeast of
Anstruther, is the prettiest of the Neuk of Fife villages,
with many **traditional houses** showing features such as
crow-step gables and pan-tiled roofs. Among the oldest
buildings here are the **Colegiate Church**, dating from
the 13th century, and a 16th-century **Tolbooth**, now
the Town Hall, outside which stands a medieval stone
Mercat Cross, crowned by a unicorn.

Adjacent to the Town Hall, the small **Crail Museum
and Heritage Centre** is an interesting guide to the
history of Crail and its surroundings.

St Andrews

Nowadays best known as the **home of golf**, St Andrews was also for centuries the religious centre of Scotland, a role it finally lost in the bloody struggles of the Reformation, which left both its cathedral and its castle in dramatic ruins. St Andrews is also one of Britain's most ancient seats of learning, with one of the four oldest universities in Britain and the oldest in Scotland. This picturesque small town has a lovely location, close to Fife's eastern tip, with huge views out to sea and sweeping sandy beaches stretching for miles north of the town.

St Andrews Castle and Visitor Centre ***

At **The Scores**, on the seafront 100m (110yd) north of the town centre, the castle was besieged and destroyed during the religious wars of the 16th century. Siege tunnels dug into the rock and the infamous **bottle dungeon** are still to be seen. The castle is open daily; opening times vary.

St Andrews Cathedral **

Less than 200m (220yd) east of the castle, at **The Pends**, the shattered remains of arches and cloisters give a vivid idea of what was, in the Middle Ages, Scotland's largest cathedral. **St Rules Tower**, which still stands, can be climbed for a fantastic view. Open daily from April to September; opening times vary.

St Andrews Preservation Trust Museum **

At 12 North Street, this 16th-century cottage with its lovely sheltered garden is preserved as a reconstruction of the town's past. Open Easter, May–September daily.

Sea Life Centre **

On The Scores, 450m (500yd) west of the castle, this **marine aquarium** features a touch pool with skates and rays, dozens of denizens of the North Sea, and an outdoor seal pool. Open daily, except April.

Above: *The ruined tower of St Andrews Cathedral.*
Opposite: *A view of St Andrews and its cathedral from the harbour wall.*

GOING UNDERGROUND

At Troywood, 10km (6 miles) south of St Andrews on the A917 (signposted from the town centre), Scotland's Secret Bunker is a relic of the Cold War – a **concrete labyrinth** some 30m (100ft) underground, where the generals and politicians would have sheltered during a nuclear attack. It is open from April to October, daily 10:00–17:00.

Central Scotland at a Glance

BEST TIMES TO VISIT

Summer and early autumn are the best times to visit central Scotland, though the region can be visited year-round. Rain is likely at any time of year, and the Fife coast is noted for its bracing North Sea winds.

GETTING THERE

By air: There are no direct air services to the region, but Dundee Airport, with flights from London, is only 24km (15 miles) from St Andrews, while Edinburgh and Glasgow airports, with flights from all over the UK and Europe, are less than an hour's drive from any point in the region.
By rail: Rail services operate to all points in Strathclyde, southern and central Scotland, and north to Oban from Glasgow Queen Street and Glasgow Central stations. For timetables and routes, contact Strathclyde Passenger Transport, tel: (0141) 332 7133. Edinburgh–Dundee line passes through Fife with stops at North Queensferry, Kirkcaldy, Cupar, and Leuchars (for St Andrews). Trains also run direct to Dunfermline and Stirling from Edinburgh, and to Stirling from Glasgow and Dundee. National Rail enquiries, tel: (0345) 484 950; ScotRail bookings, tel: (0345) 550 033.
By road: The A82 is the main road west and north of Glasgow, along the north side of the Firth of Clyde and the west shore of Loch Lomond,

then north via Tarbet, Crianlarich and Tyndrum to Glencoe and Fort William, and on through the Great Glen to Inverness. The A83 forks off west to the Mull of Kintyre from Tarbet. The A8/A78 runs along the south side of the Firth and the Ayrshire coast. Buses operate throughout the region from Glasgow Buchanan Street. Scottish Citylink Coaches, Buchanan Bus Station, Glasgow, tel: (08705) 505 050. The M90 motorway runs through Fife from Edinburgh to Perth; the M80 connects Stirling with Glasgow, and the A9 connects Stirling with Perth. Buses run on all routes. Scottish Citylink Coaches, tel: (0990) 505 050.
By sea: Caledonian MacBrayne ferries sail between Lochranza and Claonaig on the Mull of Kintyre. Caledonian MacBrayne ferries also sail from Oban to Arran, Bute, Mull, Islay, Jura, Coll and Tiree. Timetables vary seasonally; tel: (01475) 650 100.

GETTING AROUND

By road: Fife Scottish Omnibuses connect all points in the region. Kirkcaldy Bus Station, tel: (01592) 416 060; St Andrews Bus Station, tel: (01334) 474 238; Dunfermline Bus Station, tel: (01383) 621249. For details of bus and rail services throughout the region, tel: (01592) 416 060; and Scottish Citylink Coaches, tel: (0990) 505 050.

WHERE TO STAY

Argyll
LUXURY
Ardanaseig, Kilchrenan, by Tainuilt, Argyll PA35 1HE, tel: (01866) 833 333, fax: (01866) 833 222. Remote 19th-century mansion in lovely gardens.
Ardfillayne, West Bay, Dunoon, Argyll, tel: (01369) 702 267, fax: (01369) 702 501. Fine 19th-century manor house hotel in large grounds.

MID-RANGE
Enmore, Hunters Quay, Dunoon, Argyll PA23 8HH, tel: (01369) 702 230, fax: (01369) 702 148. Overlooks the Clyde.
Knipoch, by Oban, Argyll PA34 4QT, tel: (01852) 316 251, fax: (01852) 316 249. A 16th-century family-run hotel with views of Loch Feochan.

Arran
MID-RANGE
Auchrannie Country House, Brodick, Isle of Arran KA27 8BZ, tel: (01770) 302 234, fax: (01770) 302 812. Mansion with rooms or chalets, indoor pool.

Stirling
LUXURY
Stirling Highland Hotel, Stirling FK8 1DU, tel: (01786) 272 727, fax: (01786) 272 289. Central; good restaurant.

MID-RANGE
Castlecroft, Ballengeich Road, Stirling FK8 1TN, tel: (01786) 474 933, fax: (01786) 466 716. Modern four-star guesthouse.

Central Scotland at a Glance

BUDGET
Cambria Guesthouse, 141
Bannockburn Road, Stirling
FK7 OEP, tel: (01786) 814 603,
fax: (01786) 813 387. Three-
star, comfortable guesthouse.

St Andrews
LUXURY
Rufflets Country House,
Strathkinness Low Road,
St Andrews KY16 9TX, tel:
(01334) 472 594, fax: (01334)
478 703. Tasteful decor and
recommended restaurant.

MID-RANGE
**Sandford Country House
Hotel**, Newton Hill, Wormit
DD6 8RG, tel: (01382) 541
802, fax: (01382) 542 136.
Situated in four acres of
garden, overlooking the Tay.

BUDGET
Abbey Cottage, Abbey Walk,
St Andrews KY16 9LB, tel/fax:
(01334) 473 727. Comfortable
18th-century cottage, garden.

WHERE TO EAT
Argyll
MID-RANGE
Loch Fyne Oyster Bar,
Clachan, Carndow, Argyll
PA26 8BL, tel: (01499) 600
217. Magnificent seafood
from the loch, worth a stop.
**Anchorage Hotel and
Restaurant**, Shore Road,
Ardnadam, Holy Loch,
Dunoon, Argyll PA23 8QG,
tel: (01369) 705 108. Pretty
gardens, lochside scenery and
imaginative Scottish cuisine.

BUDGET
The Gathering Restaurant
and **O'Donnell's Irish Bar**,
Breadalbance Street, Oban
PA34 5NZ, tel: (01631) 565
421. Excellent grub in a lively
bar which often features live
Scottish folk music.
Chatters Restaurant, 58
John Street, Dunoon, Argyll
PA23 8BJ, tel: (01369) 706
402. Serves home-made meals
and snacks, and there are
exhibits by local artists.

Arran
MID-RANGE
**Creelers Seafood
Restaurant**, The Home Farm,
Brodick, Isle of Arran KA27
8DD, tel: (01770) 302 810.
Sophisticated seafood restau-
rant in an old bothy.

BUDGET
Brodick Castle Restaurant,
Brodick, Isle of Arran, KA27
8HY, tel: (01770) 302 202.
Excellent home bakes, lunch.

Stirling
LUXURY
Scholar's Restaurant, Stirling
Highland Hotel, Stirling FK8
1DU, tel: (01786) 272 727.
Fine à la carte and table d'hôte
menu served in surroundings
of a converted old high school.

MID-RANGE
Olivia's Restaurant, Baker
Street, Stirling FK8 1NJ, tel:
(01786) 446 277. Informal
restaurant with imaginative
menu. On the castle approach.

BUDGET
Stirling Castle Restaurant,
Stirling Castle. Reasonable
prices and convenient location.

St Andrews and Fife
LUXURY
Rufflets Country House,
Strathkinness Low Road,
St Andrews KY16 9TX, tel:
(01334) 472 594.

MID-RANGE
Aithernie Restaurant at Old
Manor Hotel, Leven Road,
Lundin Links KY8 6AJ, tel:
(01333) 320 368, fax: (01333)
320 911. Imaginatively prepared local produce.

BUDGET
**St Andrews Links
Clubhouse**, West Sands
Road, St Andrews, Fife KY16
9XL, tel: (01334) 466 666.
Affordable fixed-price menu
overlooking the world-famous
golf course.

USEFUL CONTACTS
**Kingdom of Fife Tourist
Board**, 70 Market Street,
St Andrews KY16 9NU,
tel: (01334) 472 021,
fax: (01334) 478 422.
**Ayrshire and Arran Tourist
Board**, Burns House, Ayr
KA7 1UP, tel: (01292)
288 688, fax: (01292) 288 686.
**Argyll, The Isles, Loch
Lomond, Stirling and
Trossachs Tourist Board**, 7
Alexandra Parade, Dunoon,
Argyll PA23 8AB, tel: (01369)
701 000, fax: (01369) 706 085.

6
Tayside and Grampian

The **Firth of Tay** is a tidal estuary which is more than 5km (3 miles) wide in places and navigable for more than 32km (20 miles) from its mouth near Dundee to the town of Perth. The Firth of Tay and the line of the **Ochil Hills** between the rivers Forth and Tay form a natural boundary between Perthshire and Angus and the Lowlands of central Scotland and Fife. **Strathmore**, a long, wide and fertile valley, forms a swathe of farming country dotted with castles and small towns from Perth to the Lowland hinterland of the northeast coast. To the north and west of this valley, the empty Highlands of the **Grampian Mountains**, cut through by a handful of passes and some of Scotland's most scenic roads, dominate the landscape.

The eastern Grampians, also called the **Mounth**, form a wedge that divides the coastal Lowlands of the northeast from Perthshire and Angus. Here, wild, empty mountains offer some of Scotland's finest (and most easily accessible) **wilderness walking**. But the northeast is also a region of historic castles (some authentically ruined, some well preserved and some quite recently built), North Sea fishing ports, cliffs and beaches, and wooded river valleys. **Aberdeen**, the region's main city, is Scotland's third largest.

Around the city of Aberdeen and eastward along the coast of the **Moray Firth**, the countryside is much gentler and more fertile, with small fishing ports, farming towns, and many of the distilleries that produce some of Scotland's finest malt whiskies.

DON'T MISS

*** *RRS Discovery:* Captain Scott's polar exploration ship.
*** **Verdant Works:** fascinating recreation of a 19th-century jute factory.
*** **Blair Castle:** a clan chief's home set amid beautiful scenery.
*** **Dunnottar Castle:** the striking, ghostly ruin of an impregnable fortress.
** **Balmoral:** the summer holiday home of Britain's royal family.

Opposite: *The River Tay is a quick-running stream, broadening into a tidal estuary at Perth.*

PERTH AND PERTHSHIRE

Perthshire, Scotland's largest county, embraces the lovely valleys of the rivers **Tay** and **Earn** and the glens of the central Grampians. The main road to the Highlands, the A9, runs north through Perthshire's increasingly dramatic scenery, following the Tay for much of its length.

Perth **

The small market town of Perth straddles the River Tay at its highest navigable point. The river crossing made it an important town throughout Scotland's history.

Balhousie Castle, on Hay Street, houses the regimental HQ and **museum** of one of Scotland's most venerable regiments, the **Black Watch** (Royal Highland), also called the 42nd. At Marshall Place on South Inch, the **Fergusson Gallery**, in a converted 19th-century water tower, highlights the work of the Scottish Colourist J D Fergusson. The 15th-century **St John's Kirk** is on St John Street.

Tayside & Grampian

Scone Palace ***

Scone, 3km (2 miles) north of Perth on the A93, was the seat of the Kings of Scots until the reign of Malcolm III Ceann Mor in the 11th century. The present palace dates from 1803 and houses a superb display of china, furniture, tapestries and portraits, glassware and 18th-century clocks. Open Easter to mid-October; times vary.

Dunkeld *

Dunkeld is a lovely small town, dominated by the north-west tower of its 15th-century **Cathedral**. A fine **bridge**, built by Thomas Telford in 1809, crosses the Tay here.

Pitlochry *

Pitlochry is a popular tourist town, and rather over-priced. Just to the south of the town centre, **Blair Athol Distillery**, where **Bell's whisky** is made, is an attractive complex of old buildings around a central courtyard.

Blair Castle **

About 11km (7 miles) north of Pitlochry, this is one of Scotland's most picturesque castles, with its white turrets and narrow windows. The oldest part, **Cumming's Tower**, dates from 1269. The castle is the seat of the Duke of Atholl, chief of the Clan Murray, who is the only Briton permitted to retain a private army, the Atholl Highlanders. The castle has a fine collection of arms and armour, Jacobite regalia, portraits, lace and furnishings. Open April–October, daily 10:00–18:00.

Aberfeldy *

Close to the source of the Tay, Aberfeldy is a pretty small town amid wooded slopes, less than 8km (5 miles) from Loch Tay and with excellent salmon and trout fishing and watersports nearby. **Wade's Bridge**, just north of the town, is

---

THE STONE OF DESTINY

Kenneth MacAlpin, first king of Scotland, brought the coronation stone called the Stone of Destiny to Scone around 843. Even after Malcolm III moved his capital south, Scottish monarchs continued to be crowned here, until in 1296 the Stone was seized by Edward I and taken to Westminster Abbey, where it was placed beneath the coronation throne to signify England's hegemony over Scotland. There it stayed until 1950, when it was stolen by dedicated Scottish nationalists; it was eventually recovered but returned to Scotland in 1998, a symbol of renewed nationhood.

Below: *Blair Castle, seen in the distance, is one of Scotland's most picturesque.*

named after General Wade, whose systematic building of roads and bridges in northern Scotland was the key to the pacification of the Highlands. A video presentation tells the story of **Aberfeldy Water Mill**, a working oatmeal mill on Mill Street. Tours underline the importance of mills and millers to Scottish rural life.

At **Weem**, about 2km (1.5 miles) west of Aberfeldy on the B846, is the striking 16th-century **Castle Menzies**. It houses a small clan museum.

DUNDEE AND ANGUS

Dundee, Scotland's fourth largest city, is near the mouth of the Firth of Tay. Declared a Royal Burgh in 1191, Dundee boomed during the 19th century thanks to worldwide demand for the products of its weaving mills, which produced first cotton, then jute textiles. Its whaling fleet and its shipbuilding industry were also important.

Few cities command such outstanding views, and from the top of **Dundee Law**, the long-extinct volcanic outcrop around which the city is built, you can see far northward to the Grampian ranges, often snow-capped in winter, south over the hills and coasts of Fife, westward over the Firth of Tay to Perth and far out to sea.

Two of Britain's longest bridges – the **Tay Road Bridge** and the **Tay Railway Bridge** – span the Firth of Tay at Dundee, connecting the city with Fife and the south, and carrying the main east coast road and rail routes. Angus, the district surrounding Dundee, is a region of surprising variety. Picturesque glens, within 30 minutes' drive of the city, stretch into the open spaces of the Grampian Highlands; attractive small towns and historic castles stand among the rich farming country of Strathmore; and sweeping sandy beaches and lowering cliffs adorn the North Sea coast.

Dundee

Discovery Point ***

The masts of the Royal Research Ship *Discovery* are a landmark on the **Dundee waterfront**, and the century-old vessel forms the hub of this exciting, innovative visitor attraction, with an exhibition and audiovisual display about **polar exploration** from its beginnings to the present day, as well as Polarama, an interactive science and geography gallery. Open daily; hours vary.

Frigate *Unicorn* ***

Moored in Victoria Dock, east of the Tay Road Bridge approach road, the 46-gun frigate *Unicorn*, built in 1824, is the oldest British-built warship afloat.

Above: *The 'silvery Tay' meets the sea at Dundee and is spanned by two of Britain's longest bridges.*

Verdant Works ***

Jute made Dundee's fortune, employing 50,000 people – more than half the workforce – at its 19th-century peak. Verdant Works, one of the last mills, has been restored as a **museum** and **memorial** to the industry's workers. Taped voices of the last generation of workers recalling life in the mill are fascinating and moving. Open daily; hours vary.

Dundee Contemporary Arts ***

Opened in 1999 at 152 Nethergate in the city centre, DCA is Scotland's leading contemporary arts centre. Housed in a striking building designed by Edinburgh architect Richard Murphy, it shows work by world-class artists, fosters Scottish talent, and has an excellent cinema. Open daily.

Camperdown House, Country Park and Wildlife Centre *

Built in 1828 for the first Earl of Camperdown, the graceful mansion in the Classical style stands in 160ha (395 acres) of wooded parkland. The small wildlife centre nearby has a collection of Scottish wildlife and domestic animals and delights children. Open daily; hours vary.

THE ABLE SEAMAN

Admiral Adam Duncan (1731–1804), born at Lundie near Dundee, was one of 18th-century Britain's greatest naval commanders, and would be better known were he not overshadowed by **Lord Nelson**. Commander of the North Sea fleet from 1795–1801, Duncan almost single-handedly quelled the Royal Navy mutiny of 1797, aided by his height – at 6ft 4 inches, he towered over any man in his command. In the same year, at the most crucial point of Britain's war with France and its allies, he defeated a Dutch fleet off Camperdown on the Dutch coast, a victory which was as important as Nelson's at Trafalgar, and was rewarded with the title of **Viscount Duncan of Camperdown**.

Above: *Glamis Castle, birthplace of HM the Queen Mother and setting for Shakespeare's Macbeth.*
Opposite: *The harbour at Arbroath, famous for its smoked haddock.*

Broughty Castle Museum **

At Castle Green on Broughty Ferry Harbour, 6.5km (4 miles) east of the city centre, this small castle was built during the 15th century to guard the ferry harbour and the Firth of Tay. The most interesting exhibits in the museum include whaling harpoons, photographs and model ships. Open daily; hours vary.

Claypotts Castle *

This tiny castle at Claypotts Road off the A92 on the eastern outskirts of the city is one of the finest examples of a 16th-century **laird's tower house**, with round tower, small windows and crow-step gables. Open daily; times vary.

Glamis **

Just 8km (5 miles) southwest of Forfar on the A94, this village is noted as the setting for a Shakespearean tragedy, and a 17th-century castle. **Glamis Castle** was the birthplace of HM Queen Elizabeth, the Queen Mother, and the location in Shakespeare's *Macbeth*. Supposedly haunted, it houses fine porcelain, furniture and tapestries. At Kirk Wynd in the village centre, the **Angus Folk Museum**, in a row of stone-tiled 19th-century farm workers' cottages, is packed with relics of life on the land in bygone times.

Kirriemuir **

Famous as the birthplace of *Peter Pan* creator J M Barrie, Kirriemuir is an attractive, old-fashioned town of quaint red sandstone buildings at the gateway to the Angus glens.

Forfar *

The county town of Angus, Forfar lies 16km (10 miles) north of Dundee on the A90, and is little more than a residential outpost of Dundee. About 2km (1.5 miles) northeast of town on the B9113, the square tower of the 12th-century **Restenneth Priory** stands amid the ruins.

THE BOY WHO GREW UP

James Matthew Barrie (1860–1937), son of a hand-loom weaver, was born in Kirriemuir and educated at Glasgow, Dumfries and at Edinburgh University, becoming first a journalist, then a **novelist** and **playwright**. Continuously successful throughout his lifetime, he is remembered as the author of *Peter Pan*, first performed in 1904. Constantly revived, the story of the boy who never grows up has inspired dozens of stage and film versions. Barrie was knighted in 1913.

Brechin *

A small commercial and agricultural town situated
about 12km (8 miles) east of Forfar on the A90, Brechin
was a noted medieval religious centre. Its possession of a
Cathedral allows Brechin to claim that it is Scotland's
smallest city. The attached **round tower**, dating from the
12th century, is one of only two of its kind in mainland
Scotland. It is open daily.

Arbroath *

Famed for a 14th-century compact by which Scotland
asserted its independence, and later for the delicate
flavour of its smoked haddock ('Arbroath smokies'),
Arbroath, some 36km (22 miles) north of Dundee, is an
attractive fishing port whose fleet is steadily dwindling
as the North Sea fishery declines.

At Abbey Close in the centre of Arbroath, little is
left of the Abbey but the red sandstone remnants of
its walls and arched doorways and the more complete
residence of its abbot. Immediately to the north of the
harbour, a signposted path leads to the spectacularly
weathered red sandstone cliffs with sweeping views
along the coast and out to sea.

Approximately 8km (5 miles) north of Arbroath at
Lunan Bay, the stark ruined tower of **Red Castle** is very
well named, but its deep red stone is now thoroughly
eroded by wind and water.

ANGUS COASTAL ROUTE

From Dundee, the 93km
(58-mile) Angus Coastal
Route hugs the North Sea, a
varied coastal landscape of
rugged sandstone cliffs like
those at Arbroath and
Stonehaven, or long stretches
of deserted sandy beach at
Carnoustie, Lunan Bay or
St Cyrus. Castles, fine golf
courses, nature reserves and
fishing villages are scattered
along the stretch of road to
Aberdeen and the northeast.

**THE DECLARATION OF
ARBROATH**

In 1320 the barons and earls
of Scotland met at Arbroath
for a stirring affirmation of
Scotland's freedoms in an
appeal to the Pope not to
support Edward II's claim to
Scotland. Remarkably for that
feudal era, it placed the rights
even of a Scottish king below
the liberty of his people, as
well as affirming their right
to overthrow an unjust
monarch. It concludes with
stirring defiance: '...as long
as but a hundred of us
remain alive, never will we in
any conditions be brought
under English rule. It is in
truth not for glory, nor
riches, nor honours that
we are fighting, but for
freedom – for that alone,
which no honest man gives
up but with life itself.'

DEESIDE AND THE NORTHEAST

The River Dee, which meets the sea at Aberdeen, flows from the Grampians through the northeast's scenery. The region has been a favourite holiday spot for Britain's royal family since Queen Victoria made Balmoral her Scottish hideaway. Braemar is also the base for some of the finest walking in the bare **Cairngorm Mountains** to the north and the equally dramatic, more accessible peak of **Lochnagar** (1155m/3789ft) that looms above Deeside.

Braemar **

The pretty town of Braemar is the gateway to Deeside and venue for the annual **Royal Highland Gathering**. On the banks of the Clunie Water, which flows into the Dee at Braemar, stand the earthworks of **Kindrochit Castle**, built in the 11th century by Malcolm Canmore. **Braemar Castle**, outside Braemar on the A93, is a miniature fortress with battlements and turrets. It was was rebuilt in 1748 as an army garrison on the site of an earlier castle.

Balmoral Castle **

At Crathie, 15km (9 miles) east of Braemar on the A93, Balmoral typifies the Victorian longing to recreate the fictional Scotland of Sir Walter Scott's romances. Used by the royal family since the mid-19th century, its enormous ballroom houses an exhibition of portraits, paintings and antiques. Open May–July, Monday–Saturday 10:00–17:00.

Royal Lochnagar Distillery **

About 3km (2 miles) south of Crathie on the B976, the distillery's visitor centre highlights its long royal connection as supplier of single malt whiskies to the royal family since 1848. Open Monday–Saturday; hours vary.

Banchory *

Banchory is a pleasant small market town on the River Dee, 24km (15 miles) west of Aberdeen, with several interesting historic buildings nearby. The **history museum** housed in the library has a collection of Victorian china, silverware and traditional Highland dress.

Crathes Castle **

Only 3km (2 miles) east of Banchory on the A93, this is an authentic example of a baronial castle, completed in 1596 by the local lairds, the Burnetts of Leys, and little altered. Note the fine painted ceilings in the bedrooms. The castle stands in lovely 18th-century formal gardens. Open April–October, daily 11:00–18:00.

Drum Castle **

Approximately 8km (6 miles) east of Banchory on the A93 at Drumoak, this castle is one of Scotland's oldest baronial homes. A 17th-century mansion adjoins the tower. Open May–October; opening times vary.

Stonehaven *

A small fishing harbour overlooking the North Sea, Stonehaven is known for its **Hogmanay** procession (New Year's Eve in Scotland), when flaming balls of pitch are paraded through the town.

Dunnottar Castle ***

Standing on a superb defensive site on a crag high above the North Sea, Dunnottar was built in the late 14th century and was finally destroyed after the 1715 Jacobite rising. Open year-round; days and times vary.

> **DEESIDE TOURIST ROUTE**
>
> This route takes you through the heartland of the Tayside and Grampian regions, from **Perth** and the Tay valley through the fertile farmlands of Strathmore (with the ramparts of the Grampians close on the horizon) and then deep into the hills on Britain's highest main road, via Glenshee to Braemar and Royal Deeside, and passing through Ballater, Aboyne and Banchory. The route ends at **Aberdeen**.

Below: *Balmoral Castle was the favoured Highland retreat of Queen Victoria and typifies the Victorian love of Highland romance.*

Above: *The bridge that crosses the River Tay at Dunkeld was built by Thomas Telford.*
Opposite: *The Old Bridge of Dee, outside Aberdeen, was built in 1520.*

ABERDEEN AND AROUND

Aberdeen became Scotland's third largest city in the late 1970s, boosted by the North Sea oil boom. Nicknamed **Granite City** for the silvery local rock used in many of its older buildings, it is still a major fishing harbour, with hundreds of tons of fish landed daily and auctioned early each morning at the fish market off Market Street.

St Machar's Cathedral **

A landmark in Old Aberdeen, the grand, plain 15th-century building is typical of local architecture of its period. Twin towers dominate the west front, and within is a fine ceiling painted with heraldic crests.

Kirk of St Nicholas **

Parts of this church on Union Street date from the 12th century, the vaulted lower church from the 15th century. Open May–September, Monday–Saturday; hours vary.

Provost Ross's House **

This 16th-century building on Shiprow, near the harbour, houses Aberdeen's **Maritime Museum**, full of models, artwork, and audiovisual displays of ships and shipbuilding. Open Monday–Saturday, 10:00–17:00.

King's College **

Aberdeen's university is one of Britain's oldest. Founded in 1494, King's College on the High Street is its oldest building. Its 17th-century **tower** has a distinctive crown, and a high point is the 16th-century **chapel** with its fine carved woodwork. Open daily, 09:00–17:00.

Old Bridge of Dee *

Spanning the Dee south of the town centre, just off the A90, this fine bridge, built in 1520, has seven arches, each carved with heraldic crests, and is 130m (426ft) long.

FOSSIL FUELS

The **whalers** of Scotland's east coast played their part in driving the cetaceans, first of the Arctic then the Antarctic, to the edge of extinction. Peterhead, to the north of Aberdeen, and Dundee were the home ports for huge whaling fleets. Whales were chiefly hunted for their **oil**, which until well into the 19th century was in great demand as a lubricant for machines and a fuel for lamps.

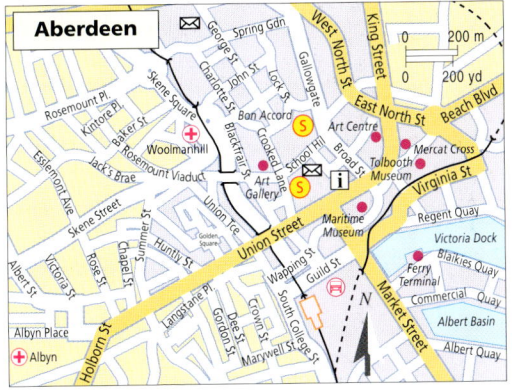

HIGHLAND TOURIST ROUTE

The 189km (118-mile) Highland Tourist Route starts at **Aberdeen** and finishes at **Inverness**, passing through the beautiful valley of **Upper Donside** and the heather-covered hills of the **Lecht** (one of Scotland's top ski spots in winter) to **Tomintoul** on the edge of the Cairngorms. This is one of the centres of whisky distilling. From Tomintoul, the route takes you into the very heart of **Speyside**, with its famed salmon fishing, and then proceeds via **Grantown-on-Spey** to Inverness, gateway to the Highlands.

Cullerlie Stone Circle *

Roughly 20km (13 miles) west of Aberdeen and 1.6km (1 mile) south of Garlogie on the B977, an enigmatic circle of eight great stones surrounds eight smaller stone cairns. The site dates from between 1000 and 2000BC.

Archaeolink Prehistory Park **

Just 13km (8 miles) west of Inverurie village and about 48km (30 miles) northwest of Aberdeen, signposted off the A96, Archaeolink reconstructs the era of the Picts and earlier dwellers in the region with film and re-enactments. Open daily, 10:00–17:00.

Castle Fraser **

Signposted from the A944 at Dunecht, 25km (16 miles) west of Aberdeen, this is the finest baronial tower house in the region, with one square and one round tower. Completed in 1636, its exterior has been changed very little since then. Open May–September daily; times vary.

Fraserburgh **

The busy fishing port of Fraserburgh looks north and east over the windswept Moray Firth and the North Sea. On **Kinnaird Head**, overlooking the port, Scotland's **Lighthouse Museum** stands next to one of the country's first lighthouses, built in 1787.

Tayside and Grampian at a Glance

BEST TIMES TO VISIT

Summer and early autumn
(June–September) are the
best times for touring and
open-air activities such as hill-
walking, fishing and canoeing.
Royal Deeside is crowded in
July and August. Skiing is
possible from December to
March and even April.

GETTING THERE

By air: International flights go
to Aberdeen from European
cities including Amsterdam,
Brussels, Copenhagen and
Paris. There are flights from
London and other major
UK cities to Aberdeen, and
flights from London to
Dundee. Aberdeen
International Airport, tel:
(01224) 722 331; Dundee
Airport, tel: (01382) 643 242.
By road: Main roads to the
region are the M90, connecting Perth with Edinburgh, and
the M80/A9, connecting Perth
with Stirling and Glasgow. The
A9 continues north from Perth
via Pitlochry and Aviemore to
Inverness. The A90 links Perth
and Dundee; the A92 runs
between Dundee and
Aberdeen; and the A98 Moray
Firth coast road links Aberdeen with Inverness. Frequent
coach services connect towns
and villages on these routes.
By rail: Trains run from
Glasgow to Perth, and from
there north to Inverness and
northeast to Dundee and
Aberdeen. From London via
Edinburgh, trains run to Perth

and on to Inverness, and
direct via Fife to Dundee and
Aberdeen. The main operators
are GNER, tel: (0191) 261
1236, and ScotRail, tel: (0141)
335 4260. ScotRail also runs
overnight sleeper services
from London to Dundee, Perth
and Aberdeen.
By sea: P&O Scottish Ferries
sail from Aberdeen to
Stromness in Orkney and to
Lerwick in Shetland; tel:
(01224) 572 615, fax:
(01224) 574 411.

GETTING AROUND

Dundee, Perth and Aberdeen
all have municipal bus services.
Local buses from these major
towns serve all points
throughout the region. Taxis
operate in all main towns and
also run between cities, larger
towns and villages.

WHERE TO STAY

Dundee and Angus
LUXURY
**Carnoustie Golf Course
Hotel**, The Links, Carnoustie
DD7 7JE, tel: (01241) 411
999, fax: (01241) 411 998.
Four-star hotel next to
Carnoustie Championship golf
course, fine views, health spa
and pre-bookable tea-times
on the golf course.
Letham Grange Hotel,
Colliston, by Arbroath DD1 4RL,
tel: (01241) 890 373, fax:
(01241) 890 725. Victorian
mansion with 20 bedrooms,
great views of its own two golf
courses, and fine restaurant.

BUDGET
Strathdon Guesthouse, 277
Perth Road, Dundee DD2 1JS,
tel/fax: (01382) 665 648.
Comfortable, family-run three-
star guesthouse in Dundee's
west end, many rooms with
lovely river views.

Perthshire
LUXURY
**Dunfallandy Country House
Hotel**, Logierait Road,
Pitlochry PH16 5NA, tel:
(01796) 472 648, fax: (01796)
472 017. Georgian mansion
on its own estate just outside
Pitlochry, with four-poster
beds, log fires and great views.
Parklands Hotel,
St Leonard's Bank, Perth
PH2 8EB, tel: (01738) 622 451,
fax: (01738) 622 046. Overlooking South Inch Park close
to the centre of Perth and the
River Tay, this is a comfortable
four-star hotel in a dignified
19th-century building with
modern rooms and facilities.

MID-RANGE
Salutation Hotel, 34 South
Street, Perth PH2 8PH, tel:
(01738) 630 066, fax: (01738)
633 598. Stylish three-star
hotel, one of the oldest in
Scotland, on Perth's main
street. Restaurant, two bars.
Dalmunzie House Hotel,
Spittal of Glenshee,
Blairgowrie, Perthshire, tel:
(01250) 885 224, fax: (01250)
885 225. Country house hotel
in picturesque baronial house,
with Scottish cooking.

Tayside and Grampian at a Glance

Birnam House Hotel, Dunkeld PH8 0BQ, tel: (01350) 727 462, fax: (01350) 728 979. This pleasant one-star hotel at Birnam, just outside Dunkeld, has a good restaurant.

BUDGET
Highland Guesthouse, 47 York Place, Perth PH2 8EH, tel/fax: (01738) 638 364. A family-run, one-star establishment situated close to the bus and train stations as well as the city centre.

Aberdeen and Northeast
LUXURY
The Marcliffe at Pitfodels, North Deeside Road, Aberdeen AB15 9YA, tel: (01224) 861 000, fax: (01224) 868 860. An excellent five-star hotel set in eight-acre grounds with 42 luxury rooms, two restaurants, and with golf and fishing nearby.

MID-RANGE
Old Mill Inn, South Deeside Road, Maryculter, Aberdeen AB12 5FX, tel: (01224) 733 212, fax: (01224) 732 884. Family-run country inn with an excellent restaurant.
Raemoir House, Raemoir, Banchory AB31 4ED, tel: (01330) 824 884, fax: (01330) 822 171. Set amid 3500 acres of Deeside parkland, with blazing fires and rooms crammed with antiques, this gracious baronial mansion is superb value for money.

BUDGET
Hamilton Guesthouse, 22 Hamilton Place, Aberdeen AB15 4BH, tel: (01224) 644 619, fax: (01224) 648 660. Family-run three-star guest-house close to the city centre.

WHERE TO EAT

Dundee and Angus
MID-RANGE
Jute Café at Dundee Contemporary Arts, 152 Nethergate, tel: (01382) 432 281. This excellent café-bar is a favourite Dundee meeting place with an imaginative menu.
Agacan, 121 Perth Road, tel: (01382) 644 227. Turkish restaurant, great food and atmosphere, original art.

BUDGET
The Deep Sea, 27 Nethergate, no tel. Dundee's best fish and chip shop, with meals to eat in or take away.

Perth
LUXURY
Exceed, 65 South Methven Street, Perth PH1 5NX, tel: (01738) 621 189. Award-winning restaurant serving stylish Scottish cuisine with cosmopolitan influences.

MID-RANGE
Let's Eat, 77/79 Kinnoull Street, Perth PH1 5EX, tel: (01738) 643 377. City-centre bistro has won several awards for consistently high standards.

Aberdeen
LUXURY
Balgonie Country House. Fresh salmon, seafood from the east coast and Orkney, superb game and Aberdeen Angus beef are highlights of this award-winning hotel restaurant.
The Courtyard on the Lane, Alford Lane, Aberdeen AB1 1YD tel: (01224) 213 795. Fish, poultry and game.

USEFUL CONTACTS

Aberdeen and Grampian Tourist Board, 27 Albyn Place, Aberdeen AB10 1YL, tel: (01224) 637 727, fax: (01224) 581 367.
Angus and Dundee Tourist Board, 21 Castle Street, Dundee, tel: (01382) 527 527, fax: (01382) 527 550.
Pertshire Tourist Board, Lower City Mills, West Mill Street, Perth PH1 5QP, tel: (01738) 627 958, fax: (01783) 630 416.

GRAMPIAN	J	F	M	A	M	J	J	A	S	O	N	D
AVERAGE TEMP. °C	10.4	11	13.2	16.3	19.1	22.4	22.9	22.1	20.6	17.3	13.5	11
AVERAGE TEMP. °F	50.7	52	55.8	61.3	66.3	72.3	73.2	71.8	69	63.1	56.3	52
HOURS OF SUN DAILY	1.7	2.7	3.4	5	5.6	6	5.2	4.7	3.9	3.1	2.1	1.5
RAINFALL mm	77	57	54	51	62	54	79	83	66	78	80	80
RAINFALL in	3	2.5	2	2	2.5	2	3.1	3.5	2.6	3.1	3.2	3.2

7
The Highlands

The Highlands of Scotland are as much a state of mind as a geographical region. Empty glens and remote lochs, beautiful snow-capped mountains and deserted beaches are the elements of the romantic Scotland of which so many visitors dream.

A wedge of mountains – the **Grampian Highlands** – thrusts south almost as far as Glasgow in the west and deep into eastern and central Scotland. In the first half of the 18th century, a string of garrison towns was built along the Great Glen, a rift valley that runs diagonally between Oban and Inverness, as part of the final pacification of the turbulent Highland clans. The journey along its chain of lochs, sea lochs and rivers, linked by the cuts and lochs of the **Caledonian Canal**, is one of the most dramatic and romantic in Britain.

Lying just south and east of the Great Glen, the mountainous regions of **Lochaber** and **Badenoch** were the setting for some of the most stirring and tragic events of Highland history. Today, their peaks and glens offer fine outdoor pursuits within easy reach of Scotland's big cities.

Scotland's Atlantic coast is fringed by dozens of fjord-like sea lochs, while inland the steep-sided glens, fast-flowing rivers, freshwater lochs and peat bogs are characteristic of one of Europe's last wildernesses.

North of the Moray Firth, the east coast is less immediately striking than the west, but the road to John O'Groats, the northernmost village in mainland Britain, has a sweeping grandeur that is all its own, as does the bleak, barren and sparsely inhabited north coast.

TOP ATTRACTIONS

*** **Culloden Moor, Inverness:** scene of the last battle fought on British soil.
*** **Loch Ness:** do monsters lurk in its murky depths?
*** **Eilean Donan Castle:** romantic ruin familiar from films and posters.
*** **Torridon:** the loveliest landscapes in Scotland.
** **Castle Sinclair:** ruined stronghold of a Norman earl.
* **John O'Groats:** northernmost village in Britain.

Opposite: *Waterfalls, rivers and mountains make the scenery of the Highlands some of the loveliest in the world.*

HEAVY METAL

An unlikely site for heavy industry, Kinlochleven stands among loch and mountain scenery. Its sole visitor attraction celebrates an early attempt to bring manufacturing jobs to a region where most people were traditionally employed in fishing, farming and fighting. At Linnhe Road, the **Aluminium Story Visitor Centre** has an exhibition and audiovisual display tracing the history of aluminium smelting in the Highlands from the early part of the 20th century.

FORT WILLIAM AND LOCHABER

Once a garrison town, Fort William, situated at the southern end of the Great Glen and the Caledonian Canal, is surrounded by magnificent sea and mountain scenery and is the best base for exploring the Lochaber region and other points further north.

Glencoe **

The A82, the main north-south highway through Argyll and the southern Highlands, passes through Glencoe, one of Scotland's most beautiful glens and the scene of the notorious massacre in 1692. Glencoe also has unique geological formations and is an important botanical site. The glen is overlooked by Aonach Dubh, high on the shoulder of which is Ossian's Cave, linked with legends of the warrior-bard of the ancient Celtic world. A visitor centre provides information on walks, with a video programme on the **Massacre of Glencoe** and a display on the **history of mountaineering** in Scotland.

Fort William **

On Cameron Square in the centre of Fort William, the **West Highland Museum** houses a fascinating collection of folk exhibits, Jacobite relics, clan tartans and weapons from fancy silver-mounted Doune pistols to brutal-looking Lochaber axes.

Ben Nevis Distillery and Visitor Centre, Lochy Bridge **

Just 3km (2 miles) north of Fort William centre, this working distillery offers an amusing **audiovisual show**, tour of the stills and **whisky tastings**. Open Monday–Friday (also on Saturday from April to September), 09:00–17:00.

Highlands

Ben Nevis ***

Britain's highest summit at 1343m (4406ft) is accessible from several approaches. The ascent generally regarded as the easiest starts from the visitor centre approximately 2.5km (1.5 miles) down Glen Nevis. Another popular ascent starts from the head of Glen Nevis, roughly 11km (7 miles) southeast of Fort William. The best view of the mountain from the town is the view from Gairlochy Road, located on the northern side of the Caledonian Canal.

Nevis Range and Aonach Mor ***

The mountain **cable car** that departs from Torlundy, about 8km (5 miles) to the north of town on the A82, takes you almost halfway to the top of Aonach Mor, the 1250m (4101ft) summit adjacent to Ben Nevis. At Aonach Mor there is skiing in the winter months, mountain walking during the summer, and there are superb views throughout the year. It is open daily from January to October; times vary.

Above: *Ben Nevis, Great Britain's highest mountain summit, seen from Corpach on the west coast.*

Treasures of the Earth **

At Corpach, approximately 6km (4 miles) outside Fort William on the A830 Mallaig road, this award-winning attraction features a dazzling collection of precious and semiprecious stones from the Highlands and also from around the world. It is open daily from February to December, 10:00–17:00.

Clan Cameron Museum ***

Located at Achnacarry, near Spean Bridge, just off the A82, the Clan Cameron Museum has displays dealing with the history of the Cameron clan, their part in the Jacobite risings of 1715 and 1745, and also the later history of the local regiment of the region, the Queen's Own Cameron Highlanders.

THE MASTER BUILDER

Thomas Telford (1757–1834) was one of the great civil engineers of his time, responsible for over 1480km (920 miles) of new roads and 120 new bridges which opened up northern Scotland during the 18th and 19th centuries. The **Caledonian Canal**, his greatest engineering achievement, was not one of the most profitable, but his works earned him burial in Westminster Abbey, a high accolade.

Above: *Loch Ness, Britain's deepest lake and the alleged home of the legendary Loch Ness Monster.*
Opposite: *Inverness Castle, built in the 19th century to replace an earlier stronghold destroyed by the Jacobites in 1745, stands on a site overlooking the River Ness.*

LOCH NESS MONSTER

The Loch Ness Monster – **myth or reality**? The debate goes on, with the faithful citing sources all the way back to St Columba, and postulating everything from plesiosaurs to aliens to exotic sea mammals as an explanation. Sceptics point out that not a shred of hard evidence for the existence of an unknown creature in the depths has ever been discovered. Even the famous **surgeon's photograph** taken in the 1930s, purporting to show a long-necked beast on the surface, has been shown to be a fake. It's still a good yarn.

Commando Monument *
Situated beside the road, this statue of a battledress-clad World War II soldier commemorates the members of Britain's elite special force, created and trained in the secrecy of the Highlands.

FORT AUGUSTUS AND LOCH NESS
The most imposing of The Great Glen lochs, Loch Ness is 39km (24 miles) long, up to 1.6km (1 mile) wide in places and up to 230m (755ft) deep. Often dark and gloomy under steep mountain slopes, it would be the perfect environment for unknown monsters, should they exist. Sadly, there is not a shred of evidence that they do.

Once a strategic fortress, Fort Augustus is now little more than a village on the main road through the glen, at the south end of Loch Ness. It has great views of the loch and is a favourite base for monster-hunters.

Drumnadrochit **
This otherwise rather dull lochside village has made a very good living off the monster industry for several decades and continues to thrive by exploiting the gullible. The **Loch Ness Lodge Visitor Centre** has a wide-screen **audiovisual** show on the loch and the **monster myth**, as well as a small exhibition of pictures and local bits and pieces, and also offers echo-sounder cruises on the loch in pursuit of the monster. **Urquhart Castle** is a picturesque ruin on the shore of the loch some 3km (2 miles) south of Drumnadrochit.

INVERNESS AND AROUND

The town of Inverness is strategically located on either side of the River Ness between Loch Ness and the Moray Firth. Its location is fortunate, with the peaks of the northwest beckoning on the horizon. The **gateway to the Highlands**, Inverness is the only large town in the region. It appears surprisingly modern, with no outstanding historic buildings.

Inverness Museum and Art Gallery **

On **Castle Wynd**, the museum has striking collections of silver and other Jacobite relics including bagpipes, shields and broadswords. The museum is open from Monday to Saturday 09:00–17:00, additionally Sunday 14:00–17:00 from July to August.

Culloden Moor, Visitor Centre and Museum ***

About 8km (5 miles) east of Inverness on the B9006 road, this is the site of the final defeat, not only of the Jacobite cause but of the age-old clan system of the Highlands. By the roadside are the **Graves of the Clans**, common graves marked by headstones for each of the clans who fought for Charles Edward Stuart. The museum shows a plan of the battlefield and recounts the events of 16 April 1745. In the middle of the moor, the great **memorial cairn** was erected in 1881. Visitor Centre and Museum open February–December daily; times vary.

Clava Cairns ***

A further 8km (5 miles) east of the Culloden battlefield, a **ring of standing stones** more than 4000 years old surrounds a cluster of Stone Age burial chambers. Interpretation boards on the site give visitors some insight into these most outstanding and enigmatic of Scotland's prehistoric remains.

MORAY FIRTH DOLPHINS

The eastern coast of the Highlands is the most northerly breeding ground in Europe for bottle-nosed dolphins. One of the best places to spot them is at **Kessock Bridge**, 1.6km (1 mile) north of Inverness, and the best time is an hour or so before high tide during the summer. Several companies run dolphin-spotting cruises along the Moray Firth: contact the local tourist information centre for details of companies that operate according to accredited guidelines designed to minimize disruption of the dolphins' environment.

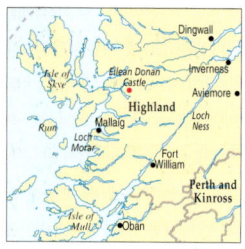

Below: *Relics of a vanished way of Highland life at one of the region's folk museums.*

THE BADENOCH HIGHLANDS

The A9 highway and the railway which follows the same route, cutting through the centre of the Grampian Highlands, is one of the most spectacular journeys in Britain. Until quite recently, the sharp curves ascending the pass known as the **Devil's Elbow** were often impassable after heavy winter snow, and even now caution should be used when driving this road in winter.

Dalwhinnie **

Dalwhinnie village, on the A9 about 64km (40 miles) south of Inverness, straddles the first of a series of mountain passes at just over 320m (1000ft) above sea level, and is best known for its **malt whisky distillery**, claimed to have the highest altitude in Scotland.

Kingussie ***

Pronounced 'Kinyoossie', this small town is a convenient stop on the main road to the north (A9). The **Highland Folk Museum** is an open-air attraction that gives visitors an insight into bygone lifestyles of the Scottish Highlands, with a farming museum, collections of traditional tools, clothes and weapons, and a reconstructed **black house** from the Isle of Lewis.

Highland Wildlife Park ***

Operated by the Royal Zoological Society of Scotland, the park offers a Highland **safari experience** through enclosures housing not only endemic species such as wildcat and otter but also animals such as bison, beaver and wolf which once roamed the Highlands. Signposted off the A9 (B9152) approximately 9km (7 miles) south of Aviemore, it is open May–October; times vary.

Aviemore *

This uninspiring purpose-built mountain activity **resort**, developed in the 1960s, is now showing its age, but has a range of medium-priced accommodation and a variety of activities from hill walking and skiing to go-karts, indoor ice rink and swimming pool.

THE WEST COAST

To the north and west of the Great Glen, the real Scottish Highlands begin: a sparsely populated region of heather-covered slopes, rugged mountains and stunningly beautiful, windswept Atlantic beaches, as well as the castles of clan chieftains.

Mallaig and Around ***

The former herring fishing port, 72km (45 miles) west of Fort William on the A830, is one of the gateways to Skye and the Western Isles, and a tourism hub for the region. On Mallaig Harbour, **Mallaig Marine World** holds local sea species as well as displays on the Mallaig fishing fleet, lifeboat and marine science.

Loch Morar ***

Southeast of Mallaig stretches the long, narrow Loch Morar, claimed to be the deepest **freshwater** loch in Britain. At around 290m (950ft) deep, it is some 65m (20ft) deeper than Loch Ness.

Eilean Donan Castle ***

Five peaks, known as the **Five Sisters of Kintail**, loom over Glen Shiel and the eastern route into Lochalsh, a wildly picturesque region of empty spaces and sea lochs. Just 15km (9 miles) east of Kyle of Lochalsh, on an islet where Loch Duich, Loch Long and Loch Alsh merge, stands the most photographed castle in the Highlands. Eilean Donan, built in 1220, was a stronghold of the Mackenzie Earls of Seaforth and their sidekicks, Clan Macrae. Held by a Jacobite garrison during the 1715 rebellion, it was demolished and has since been completely restored. Open from Easter to September, daily 10:00–18:00.

A LOST CAUSE

The A830 road west from Fort William to Mallaig passes through dramatic Highland scenery to the head of Loch Shiel, a long, narrow fresh-water loch, before reaching the west coast on the Sound of Arisaig. It was at Glenfinnan, at the north end of Loch Shiel, that **Charles Edward Stuart** raised the Jacobite standard on 19 August 1745, signalling the start of the last vain attempt to put a Stuart back on the British throne. The **Glenfinnan Monument**, erected in 1815, commemorates the clansmen who died in the Jacobite cause.

Below: *Eilean Donan Castle stands on an islet where three lochs meet.*

Above: *Loch Torridon has superb mountain scenery, ringed by peaks rising high above sea level.*
Opposite: *Ullapool, founded in 1788, is the largest town on Scotland's northwest coast.*

A WALK IN THE WOODS

More than 9000 acres of dramatic, treeless mountain-sides are gradually being reforested by the **National Trust for Scotland** with native woodland. A walking trail, once one of the cattle drovers' roads which crossed all of Scotland, leads through the **West Affric estate** and is one of Scotland's most popular hill walks. Easiest access is from **Kintail** village.

Balmacara Estate and Lochalsh Woodland Garden **

Surrounding **Lochalsh House**, this 2273ha (5616-acre) crofting estate has a woodland garden with stands of Scots pine, oak and beech, rhododendron, bamboo, hydrangeas and ferns. The little villages of **Drumbuie** and **Duirinish** are still centres for traditional crofting agriculture, and the coastal village of **Plockton**, with its quaint old-fashioned houses and superb setting, is listed as an outstanding conservation area. The estate is open all year; the woodland garden, daily from 09:00 to sunset.

Kintail and Morvich **

This 7285ha (18,000-acre) estate, located about 29km (18 miles) east of Kyle of Lochalsh off the A87, comprises the Falls of Glomach and the peaks of the **Five Sisters of Kintail**, four of which are among Scotland's highest mountains at more than 1320m (4000ft). The **Falls of Glomach**, the highest waterfall in Scotland at 123m (370ft), tumbles into a narrow gorge from a treeless mountain wilderness. The 8km (5-mile) round trip trek from Dorusduain requires five hours. The best point to start a walk to the Five Sisters is at the Countryside Centre, Morvich Farm, just off the A87 at the village of Inverinate and clearly signposted.

Torridon and Loch Torridon **

Loch Torridon, 14km (9 miles) southwest of Kinlochewe, is one of the west coast's most spectacular sea lochs. Surrounding the loch, the 6475ha (16,000-acre) Torridon Estate includes the seven tops of **Liathach**, whose highest peak rises to 1023m (3356ft), and the 922m (3025ft) Beinn Alligin. **Shieldaig Island** in Loch Torridon is a 13ha (32-acre) island covered in primeval Scots pine forest – a remnant of the forest which some 2000 years ago blanketed all of the Highlands.

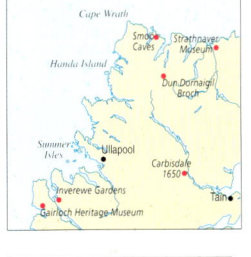

ULLAPOOL AND AROUND

Ullapool, the only town of any size in the northwest Highlands, was founded in 1788 as a **fishing port** to exploit the herring fishery and provide a livelihood for crofters driven off the land in the Highland Clearances. Located among fine scenery on the north side of **Loch Broom**, it is now a ferry port with connections to the Outer Hebrides, and a popular summer tourism base.

Ullapool Museum **

At 7 & 8 West Argyle Street, this museum highlights several aspects of the local history, telling the story of Ullapool's founding and the herring fishery. Open from March to November, Monday–Friday 10:00–17:00.

Corrieshalloch Gorge ***

This dramatic canyon through wooded cliffs, on the A835 at Braemore, 19km (12 miles) southeast of Ullapool, is 61m (200ft) deep and more than a mile long, with the 46m (150ft) **Falls of Measach** at its northern end. A viewing platform offers a fine view of the gorge and waterfall.

FLYING PESTS

One unwelcome specimen of Scottish wildlife which any summer visitor to the Highlands will encounter is the **midge**, a tiny biting fly which thrives in Scotland's damp climate and can appear in huge clouds, making summer evenings miserable for inadequately protected campers, walkers and anglers. Expose as little skin as possible, and wear insect repellent – but even then, prepare to be pestered.

Inverewe Garden ***

At **Poolewe**, approximately 60km (37 miles) southwest of Ullapool on the A832, this garden at the head of **Loch Ewe** is a remarkable sight. A uniquely mild micro-climate influenced by the Gulf Stream allows subtropical plants from all over the world to flourish throughout the year at a latitude further north than that of Moscow. Open daily; times vary.

Below: *Tartan kilts have traditionally been worn in Scotland for centuries.*

Cape Wrath and Clo Mor ***

The northernmost point on the west coast, Cape Wrath is marked by the spectacular, 280m (920ft) **sea cliffs** of Clo Mor, some of the highest in Britain.

CAITHNESS AND THE EAST COAST

To the north of Inverness and the Moray Firth, the east coast slopes diagonally in a northeasterly direction to John O'Groats, the northernmost point on the British mainland. Inland, much of the Caithness countryside is low-lying moorland or pine forest, less immediately striking than the high peaks of the northwest. North of the **Black Isle** – actually a peninsula stretching eastward into the Moray Firth – the A9 coastal highway connects a string of rather unassuming small towns, each of which has its own attractions.

Strathpeffer **

Housed in the former railway station in Strathpeffer, approximately 20km (12.5 miles) northwest of Inverness, the **Highland Museum of Childhood** brings a traditional Highland childhood to life and has a regular programme of events for children. Open from March to December; days and times vary.

Dornoch *

Dornoch, approximately 80km (50 miles) to the north of Inverness on the A9, is a quiet town facing eastwards towards the North Sea. Repeatedly restored, Dornoch's **small cathedral**, situated in the town centre, was built in 1224 by Gilbert, Bishop of Caithness, and some of its 13th-century stonework can still be seen.

Dunrobin Castle and Gardens ***

Off the A9 about 20km (12.5 miles) north of Dornoch, Dunrobin is the northeast's greatest noble castle and stately home, and is the seat of the Earls and Dukes of Sutherland. The first square keep on the site was built by Earl Robert in 1275, but the present building, in superb formal gardens, owes much of its appearance to rebuilding in the mid-19th century. Open from May to October; days and times vary.

Helmsdale *

About 120km (75 miles) north of Inverness on the A9, this town is an old herring port, with a pretty harbour. At Dunrobin Street in the village centre, displays, photographs and audiovisual presentations in the **Timespan Heritage Centre** trace Helmsdale's heritage from Viking times to the present day.

Above: *A traditional Highland crofter's house at Loch Shieldaig.*

Dunbeath *

Dunbeath, situated approximately 128km (80 miles) to the north of Inverness, has a handful of interesting sights, including one outstanding **castle**. In the Old School, **Dunbeath Heritage Centre** features an audiovisual show and tableaux of life-size figures illustrating aspects of local life and history.

Laidhay Croft Museum **

Just 1.8km (1 mile) north of Dunbeath, an early 18th-century crofting hamlet, complete with a house and byre under one roof, a barn, and a stable, furnished with contemporary tools and utensils, tells the story of the crofters of the east coast.

NORTH AND WEST HIGHLANDS ROUTE

This route takes you 224km (140 miles) through the **wildest scenery** in Scotland, passing empty glens and still lochs, coastal scenery that contrasts sandy beaches with beetling cliffs, and fishing and farming villages. Starting in **Ullapool**, it passes through the magnificent mountains of the west to Achiltibuie, Lochinver and Kinlochbervie on the way to Durness, at Scotland's northwestern tip, before turning east, along the north coast, to end at **John O'Groats**, the northernmost village in mainland Britain.

Below: *Blair Castle (see page 81) is one of seven great stately homes which can be visited on a Great Houses of Scotland pass (see also panel above).*

Clan Gunn Heritage Centre **

At Latheron, about 25km (16 miles) south of Wick on the A9 and housed in the former parish church, this centre traces the history of the **Norse Scots** of Clan Gunn to the present day. It is open from June to September, Monday–Saturday 11:00–17:00.

Grey Cairns of Camster *

These stone cairns situated some 10km (6 miles) due north of Lybster village, signposted off the A9, date from as early as 4000BC. Their purpose is unknown.

Wick **

Roughly 160km (100 miles) north of Inverness, Wick, like other settlements in this region of Scotland, was first settled by Vikings from Norway in the 8th and 9th centuries. At Bank Row, near the town centre, the **Wick Heritage Centre** has an award-winning exhibition on the life of North Sea fisherfolk and the herring industry.

Castle Sinclair and Castle Girnigoe *

The Sinclair Earls of Caithness were the descendants of Norman-Scots barons (the family name was originally St Clair) who were granted these lands by King David in the 12th century. When Orkney passed from Norway to Scotland in the 13th century, they added the islands to their realm. The twin castles of Sinclair and Girnigoe overlooking Sinclair's Bay were their strongholds – Castle Girnigoe dating from the late 15th century and Castle Sinclair from 1606–1607. The castles were both abandoned in around 1680 and have lain in ruins since the end of the 17th century.

Northlands Viking Centre **

At Auchingill, almost midway between Wick and John O'Groats, this purpose-built attraction has exhibitions about the Pictish people of Caithness before the Viking settlement, and about the Norse settlers and their rulers and their eventual integration into the nation of Scotland. Next to the centre stands a stone broch which may predate the Pictish era. Open June–September, daily 10:00–16:00.

John O'Groats *

Whether you regard John O'Groats as the culmination of your journey through Scotland or a bit of an anticlimax is up to you. At least you can say you have been there (and bought the T-shirt).

Duncansby Head and Lighthouse **

Everyone has heard of John O'Groats, but in fact the exact northernmost point of the mainland of Scotland is Duncansby Head, 29km (18 miles) north of Wick, from which you can look north to Orkney and the Pentland Skerries and south to three sandstone monoliths, the **Duncansby Stacks**, which emerge from the North Sea. Open daily from 09:00 to sunset.

Thurso *

Thurso, 20km (16 miles) northwest of Wick, is an unassuming fishing town. Scrabster, 2km (1.5 miles) north, is the ferry port for boats to Orkney. In the Town Hall on the High Street, the **Thurso Heritage Museum** contains photographs of Thurso from the 19th century to the present day, traditional crafts and tools, and a recreation of one room in an old-fashioned Caithness cottage.

The British government's tactless decision to locate Britain's first nuclear power station at **Dounreay**, 16km (10 miles) west of Thurso – as far as possible from major centres of population – prompted the Scots to ask why, if atomic energy were safe, the reactor could not be sited in the populous south of England. The site's exhibition centre presents the case for nuclear energy.

Above: *The harbour at John O'Groats, the northernmost settlement in mainland Britain.*

ON YOUR BIKE

The Scottish section of the **North Sea Cycle Route** (which spans seven countries and 9656km/6000 miles) starts with a round trip of Shetland, followed by a ferry journey to Stromness and a ride to Kirkwall before taking the ferry to John O'Groats. The route then runs along the north coast to Tongue and south to Inverness, east to Aberdeen, south to Edinburgh and on across the border to Berwick-upon-Tweed. Full details can be found on the website www.Northsea-cycle.com

The Highlands at a Glance

By air: Flights from Glasgow, Edinburgh, Manchester and London to Inverness Airport, tel: (01463) 232 471.

By road: Main roads are the A82 from Glasgow to Inverness, A9/M90 from Edinburgh via Perth to Inverness and north to Thurso, and A96 from Aberdeen to Inverness. The A87 runs west to Kyle of Lochalsh from Inverary. The A835 connects Inverness and Ullapool. Long-distance coaches from Glasgow, Edinburgh, Perth and points south to London; regional bus services to all points north and west from Inverness. National Express, tel: (08705) 010 104 or (0990) 808 080. Citylink (all services), tel: (0990) 505 050. Highland Omnibuses, regional services from Inverness, tel: (01463) 222 244.

By rail: Daily services to Inverness and Fort William from Glasgow, Aberdeen, Edinburgh and Perth, with connections to all major British cities. Overnight sleeper services between London, Inverness and Thurso. Rail services from Inverness to Kyle of Lochalsh, Thurso and Wick, and Fort William to Mallaig. ScotRail, all stations, 24hr, tel: (0345) 550 033. GNER (long-distance services, all stations), tel: (0345) 225 225.

By sea: Ferries from Mallaig to Rhum, Eigg and Muck and to Armadale on Skye, and to Barra and South Uist; and from Ullapool to Stornoway on Lewis. For all schedules and services, contact Caledonian MacBrayne, Ferry Terminal, Gourock PA19 1QP, tel: (01475) 650 100, fax: (01475) 637 607. Ferries to Orkney from Scrabster (Thurso), P&O, tel: (01224) 572 615.

Local taxis operate within and around all towns listed and can be used for longer journeys too. Local tourist offices (see Useful Contacts) can provide the numbers of reliable taxi operators. Local buses and, in remoter areas, post buses (which carry passengers and deliver mail) are alternatives to driving yourself or taking a packaged coach tour. Post Bus Service, tel: (01463) 256 273; Highland Country Buses, tel: (01463) 222 244.

Inverness
LUXURY
Dunain Park, Inverness IV3 8JN, tel: (01463) 230 512, fax: (01463) 224 532. Hotel and restaurant in Georgian manor with six suites, two cottages, four-poster rooms, superior and standard rooms, just outside Inverness on the A82. Heated indoor pool.

MID-RANGE
Glendruidh House, Old Edinburgh Road South, Inverness IV2 6AR, tel: (01463) 226 499, fax: (01463) 710 745. Victorian country house hotel on outskirts of Inverness (3km/2 miles from centre), overlooking Loch Ness Golf Course. No smoking at all.

BUDGET
Aberfeldy Lodge Guesthouse, 11 Southside Road, Inverness IV2 3BG, tel: (01463) 231 120, fax: (01463) 234 741. Comfortable guesthouse five minutes' walk from city centre.

Strathpeffer
MID-RANGE
Coul House, Contin, by Strathpeffer IV14 9EY, tel: (01997) 421 487, fax: (01997) 421 945. Family-run country house hideaway with fine wine list and acclaimed restaurant, with good fishing and golf nearby.

Tain
LUXURY
Mansfield House, Scotsburn Road, Tain IV19 1PR, tel: (01862) 892 052, fax: (01862) 892 260. Substantial Edwardian mansion, now an 18-room hotel with two restaurants. Some rooms have whirlpool bath, some have antique furnishings.

Fort William
MID-RANGE
The Lodge on the Loch, Onich, near Fort William, tel: (01855) 821 237, fax: (01855) 821 463. Fine hotel, grounds.

The Highlands at a Glance

BUDGET
The Grange, Grange Road, Fort William PH33 6JF, tel: (01397) 705 516, fax: (01397) 701 595. Victorian house in lovely garden overlooking Loch Linnhe. This is affordable luxury – Jessica Lange stayed here while filming in *Rob Roy*, on location in Glen Nevis.

Ullapool
LUXURY
Dundonnell Hotel and Restaurant, Dundonnell, Little Loch Broom, Ullapool IV23 2QR, tel: (01854) 633 204, fax: (01854) 633 366. Comfortable lochside hotel, delightfully remote, good touring base, fine restaurant.

MID-RANGE
Ardvreck Guesthouse, Morefield Brae, Ullapool IV26 2TH, tel: (01854) 612 028, fax: (01854) 613 000. Spacious rooms in modern guesthouse amid breathtaking scenery, sea views, all rooms with *en suite* accommodation.

BUDGET
Four Seasons Travel Lodge, Garve Road, Ullapool IV26 2SX, tel: (01854) 612 905, fax: (01854) 612 674. On Loch Broom, five minutes from the centre of Ullapool and two from the ferry pier, this superior bed and breakfast lodge has superb views and all rooms are *en suite* with television.

WHERE TO EAT

Inverness
LUXURY
Riverhouse Restaurant, 1 Greig Street, Inverness IV3 5PT, tel: (01463) 222 033. Small restaurant in converted Victorian building, serving fine fish, meat and game from an open-plan kitchen.

MID-RANGE
Café 1, 75 Castle Street, Inverness IV2 3EA, tel: (01463) 226 200. City-centre bistro uses high-quality local ingredients.

BUDGET
Culloden Moor Visitor Centre Restaurant, Culloden Moor, Inverness IV2 5EU, tel: (01463) 790 607. Filling soups and snacks and full meals. Self-service, non-smoking throughout.

Fort William
LUXURY
Crannog Seafood Restaurant, Town Pier, Fort William PH33 7NG, tel: (01397) 705 589. Small restaurant serving memorable local seafood in an unusual location at the end of the town pier.

MID-RANGE
An Crann, Banavie, Fort William PH33 7BP, tel: (01397) 772 077. Ten minutes' drive from the town centre, imaginative Scottish cuisine in a tastefully converted barn.

TOURS AND EXCURSIONS

Loch Ness cruises are offered by several companies such as: **Castle Cruises**, The Art Gallery, Drumnadrochit, tel: (01456) 450 695, fax: (01465) 450 205.
Jacobite Cruises, Tomnahurich Bridge, Inverness IV3 5TD, tel: (01463) 233 999, fax: (01463) 710 188.
Cruise Loch Ness, Knockburnie, Inchnacardoch, Fort Augustus, tel: (01320) 366 221.
Railtrail Tours, Glencote Park, Station Road, Cheddleton, Staffs ST13 7EE, tel: (01538) 361 334, fax: (01538) 361 118, operates five- to eight-day rail holidays in the Highlands.

USEFUL CONTACTS

Highlands of Scotland Tourist Board, Peffery House, Strathpeffer, Ross-shire IV14 9HA, tel: (01997) 421160, fax: (01997) 471168.

HIGHLANDS	J	F	M	A	M	J	J	A	S	O	N	D
AVERAGE TEMP. °C	11.2	11.2	12.8	16.6	21.5	23.5	23.3	23.3	22.7	20	17.4	12.3
AVERAGE TEMP. °F	52.2	52.2	55.1	61.8	70.7	74.3	73.9	73.9	72.9	68	63.3	54.1
HOURS OF SUN DAILY	0.9	2.2	2.9	4.4	5.3	5	3.7	3.8	2.9	2.1	1.1	0.6
RAINFALL mm	200	132	152	111	103	124	137	150	199	215	220	210
RAINFALL in	7.9	5.2	6	4.3	4.1	4.9	5.4	6	7.8	8.5	8.7	8.3

8
Western and Northern Isles

The Scottish islands are among the world's most beautiful places. Wild, remote and underpopulated, their lochs, hills, empty white-sand beaches and treeless moors are landscapes never to be forgotten. Each group of islands – indeed, each individual island – has its own unique identity, from the relatively accessible Inner Hebrides, within sight of the west coast, to the faraway Shetland archipelago, Scotland's remotest outpost, lying far out into the North Sea.

The lovely **Inner Hebrides** are the most visited of all the Scottish isles. **Skye**, the largest of the islands, is also the best known, thanks to its romantic connections to Bonnie Prince Charlie, and is also the easiest to get to, thanks to a controversial road bridge that links it with the mainland. But each of the other isles, large or small, has its own charm too.

Separated from the northwest mainland of Scotland by an often stormy channel called The Minch, the **Outer Hebrides** are islands of harshly beautiful landscapes, huge skies and lonely windswept beaches. These islands are also home to Scotland's largest remaining community of native Gaelic speakers.

The low-lying, green but almost treeless islands of the Orkney archipelago lie between 16 and 88km (10 and 55 miles) north of the Scottish mainland, from which they are separated by the Pentland Firth. Far out into the North Sea, the **Shetland archipelago** is made up of more than 100 islands, most of them tiny and uninhabited, scattered around the main island.

Don't Miss

*** Dunvegan Castle: seat of the MacLeod clan.
*** The Cuillins: Skye's most dramatic mountains.
*** Callanish Standing Stones: this ancient stone circle rivals the much more famous Stonehenge.
*** St Magnus Cathedral: superb example of medieval architecture.
** Skara Brae: evidence of the oldest settlement in Great Britain?

Opposite: *The standing stones at Callanish, erected more than 5000 years ago, are rivals to Stonehenge.*

ISLAY AND JURA

The southernmost of the Hebrides group, the two large islands of Islay and Jura are separated by the narrow **Sound of Islay**, while the 8km (5-mile) wide **Sound of Jura** separates them from the mainland. Both these

islands are famed for their strongly flavoured, dark-coloured **malt whiskies**, and distilling has traditionally been a major source of employment here.

Jura **

A long, thin island some 32km (20 miles) long by about 8km (5 miles) wide, Jura is cut almost in two by the inlet of **Loch Tarbet**, on its west coast. A single track road leads from **Kinuachdrach**, in the north, to **Feolin Ferry**, where boats cross the 500m (550yd) wide Sound of Islay to **Port Askaig**. Much of the island is trackless moorland, rising in the south to the twin peaks known as the **Paps of Jura**, some 785m (2576ft) in height. There are superb walks along the island's cliffs and beaches.

On the south coast, about 8km (5 miles) from Feolin Ferry, **Jura House Walled Garden** has a remarkable variety of shrubs and plants which flourish in the protected microclimate of the region.

Islay **

Only 500m (550yd) west of Jura, Islay is roughly crescent shaped and around 24km (15 miles) from north to south. Islay's west coast is deeply indented by **Loch Indaal** and **Laggan Bay**. More populous than its neighbour, this lovely island with its gentle landscapes is also a delight to the malt whisky connoisseur, as it produces five of the finest Scottish **malt whiskies**: Laphroaig, Lagavulin, Bunnahabhainn, Caol Ila and Bowmore.

At Bowmore, Islay's largest village on the west coast of the island, **Bowmore Distillery** is the only one of Islay's distilleries to be open to visitors without a special appointment. Bowmore has made fine whiskies using traditional methods since 1779. Guided tours and tastings are available. In the centre of Bowmore, the idiosyncratic **Round Church** was built in 1769 to an Italian design.

Colonsay *

The small island of Colonsay lies 8km (5 miles) north of Islay, with the even smaller, uninhabited island of **Oronsay** just off its southern tip. It has a handful of tiny

---

GIGHA ISLAND

Tiny Gigha, only 8km (5 miles) long by a few hundred yards wide, lies 4km (2 miles) west of the Mull of Kintyre (*see* page 67) and is one of the most charming of the islands, with even tinier satellite islands dotted around its coast. The **ruined church** at Kilchattan dates from the 13th century. Lush with flowering shrubs, **Achamore House Gardens** have been nurtured since the 1950s.

Below: *Islay is noted for its many fine malt whiskies, distilled by traditional methods in stills like this.*

MULL RAILWAY

Mull has the only railway in the islands, with narrow-gauge steam and diesel trains running between **Torosay Castle** and **Old Pier Station** at Craignure, some 24km (15 miles) south of Tobermory. The 2km (1.25-mile) trip through hills and woodlands takes 20 minutes. The railway is open Easter to October, Monday–Saturday. For the schedules, tel: (016802) 494.

fishing and farming settlements – and an 18-hole **golf course**, one of the most scenic and remote in Britain.

At **Kiloran Gardens**, situated at the northern end of Colonsay's loop of single-track road, in the grounds of **Colonsay House** (not open to the public), a forest of rare rhododendrons and other flowering shrubs flourishes in Colonsay's mild climate.

MULL

The large island of Mull, historically the territory of the Clan MacLean, lies at the mouth of **Loch Linnhe**, with **Oban** only 9km (6 miles) to the east, across the the Firth of Lorn, and the Morven Peninsula less than 3km (2 miles) to the north, across the Sound of Mull. Deep bays indent Mull's west coast, and the hilly interior rises to peaks of some 700m (2297ft) and higher. Two smaller islands, **Coll** and **Tiree**, lie to the north and west of Mull.

Tobermory **

One of the most attractive ports in the Hebrides, Tobermory is on the northeast tip of the island, on a natural harbour opening onto the **Sound of Mull**. At the western end of Main Street, situated on the harbour, the **Tobermory Distillery** offers insight into the making of malt whisky, as well as guided tours.

Below: *Duart Castle on the Isle of Mull is the seat of the chiefs of the MacLean clan, and was restored nearly a century ago.*

Duart Castle ***

Seat of the MacLean chiefs, Duart Castle was built in 1360, seized by the Campbell Duke of Argyll in 1690 when the MacLeans supported the Jacobite cause, and after 1745 was an army garrison. It was abandoned in the 18th century, and restored by Sir Fitzroy MacLean in 1911. Inside are dungeons and a museum of clan history. Open May to September, daily 10:30–18:00.

Iona ***

Just 500m west of **Fionnphort** on the western tip of Mull, Iona was the burial place of Scottish kings for centuries, and the place from which Christianity was brought by St Columba. The oldest building is **St Oran's Chapel**, built in 1080 and, like the cathedral and monastery, restored by the Iona Community. Access is by ferry from Fionnphort.

Staffa **

Approximately 9km (6 miles) north of Iona, the stark basalt columns and caves of uninhabited Staffa, where the remains of the Gaelic hero **Fingal** are reputed to lie, inspired Mendelssohn's 'Hebrides' overture. Access is by boat from Iona, from April to October.

Above: *Tobermory, Mull's island capital, is one of the prettiest island ports.*
Below: *The Hebridean islands are a favourite with yacht sailors.*

Rhum, Eigg, Muck and Canna *

Between Mull and Skye are four smaller islands which are most easily reached from Mallaig, on the mainland (*see* page 99). Canna, owned by the National Trust for Scotland, is of interest mainly to birders and naturalists. Eigg and Muck are not for sightseers, but offer natural beauty and splendid isolation. Rhum, the largest of the four, is all of 8km (5 miles) wide and dotted with steep hills rising to 700m (2150ft) and more. The entire island is a nature reserve, with seabirds, seals and red deer.

   Kinloch Castle, on Rhum, is a magnificent mansion which was built at the end of the 19th century and which still has many of its lavish Edwardian furnishings. It is now a hotel and hostel (*see* Where to Stay, page 121).

SKYE

The largest island of the Inner Hebrides – almost 64km (40 miles) from north to south and 32km (20 miles) wide at its widest. Skye is also the best known, largely on the

Above: A new road bridge links Kyleakin on the Isle of Skye with the mainland.

strength of the ballad celebrating Charles Edward Stuart's escape after Culloden, *The Skye Boat Song.* A new road bridge, much criticized by environmentalists and islanders who resent the high tolls, connects **Kyleakin**, in eastern Skye, with **Kyle of Lochalsh**. On Skye's west coast lie the **Cuillin Hills**, a range of steep-sided summits of which seven are over 900m (2953ft) high.

Armadale *
Armadale, 16km (10 miles) southwest of Kyleakin on the Sleat Peninsula, was a stronghold of the MacDonald Lords of the Isles and is surrounded by woodlands, trails and moorland walks.

Clan Donald Visitor Centre, Armadale Gardens ***
In a restored section of Armadale Castle, the **Museum of the Isles** recounts the history of the MacDonald clan and the Lords of the Isles. It stands in lovely gardens. Open April–October, daily 09:30–17:30.

Portree ***
Skye's largest village stands on a sheltered inlet opening into the **Sound of Raasay**, on the island's east coast. At Viewfield Road in central Portree, the **Skye Heritage Centre** tells the story of Skye from 1700 to the present from the point of view of the ordinary islanders.

Old Skye Crofter's House *
At **Luib**, 24km (15 miles) south of Portree on the A850 coast road, a thatched **traditional cottage** is furnished as it would have been in the early 20th century, and illustrates how little island life had changed until that time. Open daily, 09:00–18:00.

Dunvegan Castle and Gardens ***
This castle, situated at the head of **Loch Dunvegan**, has been the seat of the MacLeod chiefs for seven centuries, and the genealogical exhibition within claims to trace

30 generations of MacLeods. Also on show here are relics of **Bonnie Prince Charlie**, pictures, weapons and other family possessions. The castle is open from March to October, daily 10:00–17:30.

Colbost Croft Museum **

A further 4km (3 miles) west of Dunvegan, this low, turf-walled and thatched **black house** is typical of crofters' homes in the islands as recently as the 19th and early 20th centuries. Open daily, 10:00–18:00.

Piping Centre **

Situated directly opposite **Colbost Croft Museum**, this museum celebrates the Highland bagpipe and especially the legendary MacCrimmon family, the hereditary pipers to the MacLeod chiefs for three centuries. It is open from Easter to October, daily 10:00–17:30.

Skye Museum of Island Life **

At Hunglader on Trotternish, 32km (20 miles) north of Portree, a cluster of seven thatched cottages shows how life was in a crofting community in the mid-19th century, and includes farm tools, domestic utensils and furniture.

Quiraing **

Approximately 31km (19 miles) north of Portree, this strange natural rock formation, a cluster of basalt spires and stacks, surrounds **The Needle**, a stone column of some 37m (120ft) in height.

THE OUTER HEBRIDES

The largest of the Scottish islands is **Lewis**, almost 96km (60 miles) from **Rhenish Point** in the south-west to the **Butt of Lewis** in the northeast, and more than 48km (30 miles) across at its widest. Much of Lewis is low-lying peat moorland with hundreds of tiny lochs and tarns. The southwestern

---

TRACE YOUR ANCESTORS

There are far more people of Scots descent living abroad than there are in Scotland. For many, tracing a lost family history is a big part of a trip to Scotland. If you have a clan surname, organizations such as the **Clan Donald Centre** on Skye may give you some insight into your ancestry. In Edinburgh, **New Register House** holds most records of births, deaths, marriages, census and parish records, and you can start your detective work on their website, www.open.gov.uk/gros/groshome.htm. The **Scottish Genealogy Society** also has it own website with a list of profes-sional ancestor hunters, www.scotland.net/scotgensoc/

Below: *Dunvegan Castle on Skye has been the seat of the chiefs of the MacLeods for seven centuries.*

Above: *Impressive basalt spires and stacks surround the Needle at Quiraing, north of Portree.*

peninsula of the island, Harris, is known as the **Isle of Harris**. A separate community, until recently it was more easily reached from Lewis by sea than by road.

Stornoway **

Stornoway, Lewis's capital, is on the east coast, looking out across **Broad Bay** towards the **Eye Peninsula**, a limb of land that shelters Stornoway and its harbour and is connected to the main body of the island by a narrow isthmus. On Francis Street, the **Museum nan Eilean** traces the history of Lewis and its people from Celtic and Viking times.

Steinacleit Cairn and Stone Circle *

This mysterious ring of standing stones, about 40km (25 miles) north of Stornoway on the east coast, dates from the 3rd millennium BC.

Callanish Standing Stones ***

About 23km (14 miles) west of Stornoway, this unique collection of **megaliths** set out in the shape of the cross was constructed from 3000–1500BC and is considered to be as archaeologically important and impressive as Stonehenge. An avenue of 19 standing stones leads to a ring of 13 stones surrounding a chambered tomb.

Dun Carloway Broch **

At Carloway, 16km (10 miles) north of Callanish, this 10m (30ft) tall **Iron Age tower** or broch is one of the best preserved in the Highlands and islands.

Gearannan Village **

Only 3km (2 miles) north of Carloway, this village of traditional turf-walled **black houses** has been restored as a **living museum**.

ANCIENT PATHS

On **Harris**, a walkway project is restoring ancient pathways used by local people for at least a thousand years and probably much longer. New way-marked paths across Harris's beautiful, desolate moors and peat bogs will enable visitors to explore one of the most unspoilt places in Europe on foot, an experience not to be forgotten.

The Uists, Benbecula and Barra **

North Uist, the northernmost of a chain of four islands stretching southward from the Isle of Harris, is only 8km (5 miles) south of Rhenish Point on **Harris**. Deeply indented coastlines and hundreds of lochs and inlets make it hard to tell where each island stops and the next begins. **Benbecula**, lying between North and South Uist, is connected to both by a road bridge. Barra, the southernmost of the four, lies 12km (7 miles) from the southern tip of South Uist. With few formal visitor attractions, these are islands for island lovers, with broad, sweeping Atlantic views, sea and loch fishing, and many rare seabird species.

St Kilda ***

Loneliest of all the Scottish islands, deserted St Kilda stands far out into the Atlantic, 80km (50 miles) west of Harris. Abandoned by its last inhabitants in the 1930s, it is now a UNESCO **World Heritage Site**. At Conachair, the 450m (1476ft) sea cliffs are the highest in Britain and the nesting place for thousands of gannets, puffins, fulmars and other seabirds. Other unique wildlife includes **Soay sheep** and endemic species of mouse and wren. St Kilda is extremely hard to get to; for access contact National Trust for Scotland, tel: (0131) 226 5922.

ORKNEY

Brochs, stone circles and **earth houses** testify to early settlement of these islands, but when Norse settlers arrived in the 7th and 8th centuries they found them uninhabited. Orkney did not become part of Scotland until the 13th century, and even then its piratical Earls, the Sinclairs, paid only lip service to the Crown.

The largest of the Orkney islands, confusingly just called **Mainland**, is 32km (20 miles)

PICTS AND SCOTS

Mystery surrounds the Picts, their still undeciphered script and their carved symbolstones. Some of the most ancient buildings in Scotland, such as the brochs of the far northeast or the souterrains of Angus, were popularly believed to be built by them, though in fact they were probably the work of even earlier people. With the coming of the Scots, the Picts fade from history – not through genocide but through intermingling with the incomers, whose language, culture and appearance was probably very similar to their own.

Below: *Stornoway, capital of the Isle of Lewis, looks out across Broad Bay.*

FISHY STORIES

Did an Orcadian nobleman
see the Americas a century
before Columbus? According
to the so-called **Zeno
Narrative**, the Venetian
navigator and chronicler
Nicolo Zeno crossed the
Atlantic in 1398 in the
company of a 'prince of the
islands', identified by at least
one scholar as **Henry
Sinclair** (1345–1400), whose
voyage was inspired by the
stories of Orkney fishermen
who knew of rich fishing
grounds off the coast of
what is now Newfoundland.

from end to end, with its capital, **Kirkwall**, facing north
across a bay sheltered by the much smaller island of
Shapinsay. The island's second town, **Stromness**, on the
south coast, looks over Hoy Sound towards the neighbouring island of Hoy. Stromness has a more sheltered
harbour than Kirkwall and is Orkney's main ferry port.

Kirkwall ***

Kirkwall's broad streets and solidly built stone houses
are overlooked by the splendid spire of a 12th-century
cathedral, and from the harbour there are fine views out
to the neighbouring islands.

St Magnus Cathedral was founded in 1137 by Earl
Rognvald in memory of his uncle, Earl Magnus, the first
Orkney earl to accept Christianity. The first phase of
building was completed by the end of the 13th century,
but additions were made over the next three centuries.
One of the finest pieces of **Norman architecture** in
Scotland, it is still used as
a place of worship.

Another remarkable
piece of architecture, this
time dating from 1607 and
in fine Renaissance style,
Earl Patrick's Palace was
built for Earl Patrick
Sinclair, last of the Orkney
earls to remain virtually
an independent ruler.
Next to it, the miniature
Bishop's Palace, with its
round tower, dates from
the 13th century.

Maes Howe ***

About 8km (5 miles) east
of Stromness town centre
on the Kirkwall road, this
huge burial mound, dating
back to 2500BC, contains

Orkney Isles

one of the largest burial chambers in Europe. **Runic graffiti** inside the chamber dates from Viking times. Open daily; times vary.

Unstan Chambered Tomb *

Just 6km (4 miles) northeast of Stromness, this **prehistoric cairn** contains a 2m (6ft) high tomb chamber from which significant archaeological finds have been made. Open daily; times vary.

Ring of Brodgar ***

This very impressive circle of 36 standing stones is the nucleus of a complex of deep ditches cut into the rock, mounds and other monoliths. Its purpose is unknown. Dating from around 3000BC, there were originally 60 stones in the Ring.

Earl's Palace *

Some 18km (11 miles) north of Stromness stand the ruins of a 16th-century fortified palace of the Earls of Orkney.

SHETLAND

Mainland is some 80km (50 miles) from north to south, and its shore is deeply serrated. It has awesome views, harsh cliffs and deserted white-sand beaches. **Lerwick**, the main town and port, lies in the southern part of the island, on the east coast. Mainland and its neighbours are low lying and treeless, and the highest point, **Scalla Field**, is only 281m (750ft) in height. Settled like Orkney by Vikings during the 9th-century AD, Shetland became part of Scotland only in 1469.

Lerwick **

Solid stone houses surround the picturesque small harbour of Lerwick. The town's attractions include the small

Above: *Kirkwall's St Magnus Cathedral, built by a devout Viking earl almost nine centuries ago.*
Below: *These ruins are all that remain of the Earl's Palace at Kirkwall, dating from the 16th century.*

Above: *The wheelhouses at Sumburgh in Shetland date from the Iron Age.*

Shetland Museum, which gives fascinating insights into the five millennia of human settlement in Shetland and the 17th-century **Fort Charlotte**.

Jarlshof ***

This fascinating archaeological site at **Sumburgh Head**, 32km (20 miles) south of Lerwick, spans three millennia, from the late Stone Age of the second millennium BC up to Viking times. It comprises three separate settlements, from the neolithic, Pictish and Viking eras, as well as a medieval farm and the 16th-century mansion of the Stewart Earls of Shetland. Open daily; times vary.

SCAPA FLOW

The huge **natural harbour** of Scapa Flow, sheltered by the mainland and the neighbouring islands of South Ronaldsay, Burray, Hoy, and Flotta, was a major base for the Royal Navy in both World War I and World War II. At the beginning of World War 1 a German submarine penetrated its defences to sink the British flagship **HMS Royal Oak** with British commander in chief, Lord Kitchener, on board. In 1919 the German Imperial Fleet surrendered here, only to be scuttled by its commanders in a last act of defiance. The wrecks of these warships lie at the bottom of the Flow, making it a favoured site for **diving**.

Shetland Isles

Unst
Haroldswick
ATLANTIC OCEAN
Yell
Gutcher · Belmont
Fetlar
Mid Yell
North Roe
West Sandwick
Funzie
Otherswick
Hillswick
Toft
Out Skerries
Hamnavoe
St Magnus Bay
Brae
Lunning · Whalsay
Papa Stour · Muckle Roe
Voe
Sandness
Neap
Dale of Walls
Westerfield
South Nesting Bay
Walls
Lerwick
Scalloway
Gunnista
Scalloway
West Burra
Fladdabister
Mousa Broch
0   20 km
Sandwick
0   10 miles
Quendale
Ness of Burg
Toab

NORTH SEA

Shetland Islands

Orkney Islands

SCOTLAND

N

Western and Northern Isles at a Glance

GETTING THERE

By air: Flights from Edinburgh and Aberdeen to Shetland (Lerwick) and Orkney (Kirkwall), and flights from Glasgow to Lewis (Stornoway) and Barra.
By sea: Caledonian MacBrayne Ferries to 22 west coast islands from Mallaig, Oban, Ullapool, tel: (01475) 650 100, fax: (01475) 637 607. P&O Scottish Ferries from Aberdeen to Orkney (Stromness) and Shetland (Lerwick), tel: (01224) 572 625, fax: (01224) 574 411. Ferries from John O'Groats to Orkney (Burwick), tel: (01955) 611 353, fax: (01955) 611 301.

GETTING AROUND

For Inner Hebrides and Western Isles, *see* Caledonian MacBrayne (above). In Orkney, contact Orkney Ferries, Kirkwall, tel: (01856) 872 044, fax: (01856) 872 921. Shetland Islands Council, Lerwick, tel: (01806) 244 234, fax: (01806) 244 232, operates Shetland inter-island services.

WHERE TO STAY

Skye
LUXURY
Cuillin Hills Hotel, Portree, Isle of Skye IV51 9QU, tel: (01478) 612 003, fax: (01478) 613 092. Superb location, fine food and delightful rooms, plus many outdoor activities.

Kinloch Lodge Hotel, Sleat, Skye IV43 8QY, tel: (01471) 833 333, fax: (01471) 833 277. The home of Lord and Lady MacDonald, this 16th-century country house is delightful, the food superb.

MID-RANGE
Atholl House Hotel, Dunvegan, Skye IV55 8WA, tel: (01470) 521 219, fax: (01470) 521 481. Small, comfortable hotel in a converted 19th-century church manse, excellent restaurant

Lewis and Harris
MID-RANGE
Park Guesthouse, 30 James Street, Stornoway HS21 2QN, tel: (01851) 702 485, fax: (01851) 703 482. Centrally located family-run guesthouse with acclaimed restaurant.

Orkney
LUXURY
The Kirkwall Hotel, Harbour Street, Kirkwall, Orkney KW15 1LF, tel: (01856) 872 232, fax: (01856) 872 812. Orkney's best hotel, in 19th-century building on harbour.

MID-RANGE
Ayre Hotel, Kirkwall, tel/fax: (01856) 873 001. Comfortable four-star, hotel with 33 *en suite* rooms.

WHERE TO EAT

Orkney
Creel Restaurant and Rooms, Front Road, St Margaret's Hope, Orkney KW17 2SL, tel: (01856) 831 311. Historic house with three *en suite* rooms and a fine restaurant, Orcadian food.

Shetland
Burrastow House, Walls, Shetland ZE2 9PD, tel: (01595) 809 307, fax: (01595) 809 213. Modern rooms, wonderful cooking in the country.
Busta House Hotel, Busta, Shetland ZE2 9QN, tel: (01806) 522 506, fax: (01806) 522 588. Historic 16th-century mansion with private gardens and many unusual features.

USEFUL CONTACTS

Western Isles Tourist Board, 26 Cromwell Street, Stornoway, Isle of Lewis HS21 2DD, tel: (01851) 703 088, fax: (01851) 705 244.
Orkney Tourist Board, 6 Broad Street, Kirkwall, Orkney KW15 1NX , tel: (01856) 872 856, fax: (01856) 875 056.
Shetland Islands Tourism, Market Cross, Lerwick, Shetland ZE1 0LU, tel: (01595) 693 434, fax: (01595) 695 807.

WESTERN ISLES	J	F	M	A	M	J	J	A	S	O	N	D
AVERAGE TEMP. °C	7.2	7	8.3	10.3	12.7	14.8	15.8	16.1	14.7	12.6	11.5	9
AVERAGE TEMP. °F	45	45	46.9	50.5	54.9	58.6	59	61	58.5	54.7	53	48
HOURS OF SUN DAILY	1.3	2.7	3.5	5.2	6	5.8	4.1	4.3	3.3	2.3	1.5	1
RAINFALL mm	182	116	129	93	91	104	113	118	170	204	203	197
RAINFALL in	7.2	4.6	5.1	3.7	3.6	4.1	4.5	4.6	6.7	8	8	7.8

Travel Tips

Tourist Information
The **Scottish Tourist Board** (STB) has offices in London. Elsewhere in the world, tourist information about Scotland is available from the **British Tourist Authority** in Sydney, Ontario, Hong Kong, Dublin, Auckland, Singapore, Johannesburg and New York.

Entry Requirements
Valid passport required for all visitors. No visa required for citizens of EU countries or USA. Most other nationalities, including Commonwealth countries, require visas.

Customs
Visitors arriving from EU countries are not entitled to duty-free allowances, but may bring in unlimited amounts of tax-free goods for personal use. Arrivals from outside the EU may bring in 1 litre of spirits plus two litres of still table wine, 200 cigarettes or 50 cigars, 500cc perfume and gifts worth up to £150.

Health Requirements
No specific requirements are in force.

Getting There
By air: Flights from North American cities including Toronto, New York and Chicago to Glasgow. Flights from major European cities to Glasgow, Edinburgh and Aberdeen. Internal flights from major English cities to Edinburgh, Glasgow, Aberdeen, Inverness, and from London only to Dundee.

By road: Use motorways M6 (west coast) and M1 and A1 (M) (east coast) from London. The A1 (M) ceases to be a motorway at the border, but if you want to use motorway all the way from London, use the M6 (west coast) route which does connect with the Scottish motorway system at the border. Express coaches run from all British cities to Edinburgh, Glasgow, Dundee and Aberdeen.

By rail: Rail services run from London via the west coast to Glasgow and via the east coast to Edinburgh and all points north. Cars can be transported unaccompanied from London by **Motorail**, tel: (0990) 502 309, fax: (01483) 268 866, or by

Auto Shuttle Express, tel: (0990) 502 309.

By ferry: Newcastle, some 180km (112 miles) south of Edinburgh in northeast England, is the main ferry port for Scotland, with services from Amsterdam (Netherlands), Bergen, Stavanger and Kristians (Norway) and Gothenburg (Sweden). Ferries from Northern Ireland sail between Belfast and Stranraer in Ayrshire; Ballycastle and Campbeltown in Argyll; and Larne and Cairnryan. Ferries also connect Lerwick in Shetland with Torshavn in the Danish-owned Faeroe Islands and Bergen (Norway).

What to Pack
Warm, waterproof clothing and footwear are essential year-round. Gloves, hat and scarf should be added for winter trips. Hill-walkers must wear proper walking boots and also pack a waterproof cagoule and trousers, a warm sweater or fleece and full winter kit, including sleeping bag and survival bag or tent. Insect repellent is a must in

BOOKING THROUGH OSSIAN

Ossian, Scotland's pioneering tourism booking and information database, was launched in 1999 and is intended to make it possible to book virtually every aspect of Scottish tourism via the **Internet**, with up to 16,000 tourism enterprises, from tour operators to guesthouses and visitor attractions, linked to its database. Access it at: www.holiday.scotland.net

summer. A few of the five-star traditional hotels may insist on a jacket and tie for men at dinner, but generally speaking, formal wear is not otherwise needed.

Money Matters

Currency is the UK pound sterling, divided into 100 pence. Scottish banks issue their own notes in £5, £10, £20, £50 and £100 denominations, and Bank of England notes are equally acceptable. Coins are in 1p, 2p, 5p, 10p, 20p, 50p, £1 and £2 denominations. All major convertible currencies can be readily exchanged at banks and in larger cities also at *bureaux de change*, but generally not at the smaller hotels and guesthouses. All but the smallest establishments accept major credit cards. Automatic teller machines (ATMs) in all but the smallest villages issue cash advances against credit cards or Cirrus debit cards.

Accommodation

The Scottish Tourist Board grades accommodation from one to five stars according to quality rather than facilities or size. Five-star properties will be exceptional by any standards; four-star will be excellent, three-star very good, two-star good, and one-star will be fair to acceptable. Inspectors grade each property annually. Accommodation ranges from modern international chain hotels and palatial city-centre hotels dating back to the heyday of the railway age to elegant Georgian and Victorian townhouses, baronial castles and country houses, quiet fishing lodges, simple bed-and-breakfast establishments and guesthouses to budget hostels and dormitories in the countryside and in the cities. Scotland also has plenty of strategically located campsites and caravan sites. Camping in remoter areas is generally tolerated, though it is tactful to ask permission if possible.

Eating Out

There are excellent restaurants throughout Scotland. The best are clustered in major cities, especially in Edinburgh and Glasgow, but there are many fine establishments in surprisingly remote locations. For the best of Scottish produce and high culinary standards, look for the **stockpot** symbol indicating membership of the **Taste of Scotland Scheme**, with 400 members. For everyday eating

USEFUL WEBSITES

Useful tourist board websites in Scotland include:
Edinburgh
www.edinburgh.org
The Borders
www.scot-borders.co.uk
www.galloway.co.uk
Glasgow
www.seeglasgow.com
Central Scotland and Fife
www.ayrshire-arran.com
www.standrews.co.uk
Dundee, Tayside and Grampian
www.angusanddundee.co.uk
www.perthshire.co.uk
www.agtb.org
Highlands
www.host.co.uk
Islands
www.orkney.com
www.shetland-tourism.co.uk
www.witb.co.uk

most Scottish towns host a wide range of restaurants – you'll find Italian pasta and pizza houses, Indian and Chinese restaurants almost everywhere, along with steakhouses, Tex-Mex and burger joints. Seafood restaurants range from cheap and cheerful fish and chip shops where you can eat in or take your meal away, to the finest and most costly establishments. Global fast-food chains such as MacDonalds and Pizza Hut are also found around Scotland. Most pubs serve coffee, snacks and simple meals as well as drinks. Most restaurants are open 12:00–14:30 for lunch and 18:00–22:00 for dinner.

TOURIST ROUTES

You can avoid busy and rather dull main roads by detouring onto the twelve **National Tourist Routes**. Marked by signposts with white lettering on a brown background and bearing a blue thistle symbol, these follow quieter, prettier routes through the countryside and have been chosen for their scenic appeal and for visitor attractions along the way.

Most pubs and bars are open 11:00–23:00 or later from Monday to Saturday, closing at 23:00 on Sunday, but many in the towns and cities stay open until 02:00 or even later, especially on Fridays and Saturdays.

Transport

By air: There are flights from London and other major English, Irish and Welsh cities to Glasgow, Edinburgh, Aberdeen, Inverness and Dundee. There are also flights from Glasgow to Stornoway, Barra and Uist as well as from Aberdeen to Kirkwall and Lerwick.

By car: Roads vary from six-lane motorways and four-lane dual carriageways in Central and Lowland Scotland to mostly two-lane main roads north of Inverness and even single-lane roads in the northwest. Road surfaces and signage are generally good. Towns, villages and major and minor sights and attractions are clearly and frequently signposted.

Drive on the left. Speed limits are 110kph (70mph) on motorways and dual carriageways, 95kph (60mph) on other main roads, and usually 48kph (30mph) or less in towns, cities and villages unless otherwise stated. Use of seat belts in front seats and (where fitted) in back seats is compulsory. Holders of overseas driving licences may drive in the UK for up to one year. Car rental is available throughout Scotland from major international chains and local companies. Most require you to be over 23. Fuel is extremely expensive.

By bus: Scottish Citylink Coaches, Buchanan Bus Station, Killermont Street, Glasgow G2 3NP, tel: (08705) 505 050, have services to 190 destinations. The Citylink Explorer Pass allows unlimited travel for three, five, eight or 15 days. Several companies (details are available from STB/BTA) offer jump on/jump off routes round Scotland for budget travellers. In the remoter areas, mail is delivered by post buses which also take fare-paying passengers when no other transport is available. Time-tables are obtainable from the Communications Department, Royal Mail Scotland, 102 West Port, Edinburgh EH3 9HS, tel: (0131) 228 71407 fax: (0131) 228 7139.

By train: The main railway lines in Scotland are between Glasgow and Edinburgh; trains run from Glasgow via Perth to Inverness and points north, and also to Dundee and Aberdeen; and from Edinburgh via Dundee to Aberdeen and via Perth to Inverness and points north. Trains also run from Glasgow to Fort William and between Aberdeen and Inverness. For all information on rail travel within Scotland contact ScotRail, tel: (0141) 335 4260.

By ferry: Caledonian MacBrayne sails to 22 islands in the Hebrides and Firth of Clyde from ports including Oban, Gourock, Mallaig, Oban and Ullapool. Island Rover and Island Hopscotch tickets offer discounts for island-hoppers. For more

CONVERSION CHART		
FROM	**TO**	**MULTIPLY BY**
Millimetres	Inches	0.0394
Metres	Yards	1.0936
Metres	Feet	3.281
Kilometres	Miles	0.6214
Square kilometres	Square miles	0.386
Hectares	Acres	2.471
Litres	Pints	1.760
Kilograms	Pounds	2.205
Tonnes	Tons	0.984
To convert Celsius to Fahrenheit: x 9 ÷ 5 + 32		

information, tel: (01475) 650 100, fax: (01475) 637 607. Ferries also sail to Stromness in Orkney from Scrabster on the north coast and from Aberdeen, and to Burwick in Orkney from John O'Groats. Inter-island ferries operate between the various Orkney islands. There are ferries to Lerwick, in Shetland, from Aberdeen, and the Shetland Islands Council also operates inter-island ferries.

Business Hours
Shops are usually open from Monday to Saturday between the hours of 09:00 and 17:30 or 18:00. Many supermarkets in large cities stay open until 20:00 and many shops open on Sundays too. Banks are generally open 09:30–16:00 Monday–Friday.

Time Difference
GMT November to March, GMT +1 April to October.

Communications
Telecommunications in Scotland are excellent, with **telephone** booths operated by British Telecom and some of its competitors in even the smallest of villages, offering full international direct dialling and payment by credit card, by phone card or by many of the various international cut-rate systems. **Internet cafés** in all the major towns offer e-mail and Web services. **Fax services** are generally available at all the major hotels and also from most post offices and private copy shops in the small villages.

Electricity
In Scotland, use 240 AC with three-pin socket.

Weights and Measures
In theory, the metric system and Centigrade thermometer are standard. In practice, however, distances are usually given in miles, weights in pounds and beer in pints. Fuel is sold in litres.

Health Precautions
No special health precautions are necessary.

Health Services
Public health services in Scotland are good. EU citizens with form E111 will receive free medical treatment.

Personal Safety
Scotland is generally a safe and relatively low-crime country. Some areas of Glasgow, Edinburgh and Dundee, mainly areas of poor housing and high unemployment on the outskirts of cities, have relatively high crime rates, but are unlikely to be on your itinerary. As in any major city, however, be wary of bag-snatchers or pick-pockets. Keep a close eye on your possessions on public transport, and do not leave your valuables visible in unattended vehicles.

Emergencies
Police, ambulance and fire brigade, tel: **999**.

Etiquette
There are no special etiquette requirements.

FINDING A BED

It is a good idea to make bookings in advance for accommodation during July and August – the busiest time of year – and in winter, when many establishments are shut. The Book-A-Bed-Ahead (BABA) service at Tourist Information Centres throughout Scotland enables you to arrange accommodation for the next night or for several nights in advance in another area, for a £3.00 fee plus ten per cent deposit.

Language
English, albeit sometimes spoken in one of several rather impenetrable urban accents, is the standard language of Scotland. There is only a tiny minority of Gaelic speakers in the country, and they are equally fluent in the English language.

Holidays and Festivals
Scottish public holidays are generally similar to those in the rest of the United Kingdom but do not include Easter Monday, while the August bank holiday is generally at the beginning of the month, not at the end as in England. While **New Year's Day** (1 January) is a public holiday throughout the United Kingdom, the Scots also take 2 January as a holiday. St Andrew's Day (30 November), the day of Scotland's patron saint, is not actually a holiday. Several of the cities and

towns have their own specially designated 'holiday fortnight', usually at some time in August, when many of that town's shops and businesses formerly closed at the same time, but nowadays this practice is dying out. **Edinburgh's International Festival**, lasting for three weeks in August, is a world-famous celebration of entertainment and the arts. **Burns Day** (25 January), the birthday of Scotland's best known poet, is celebrated nationwide (and also worldwide) with haggis, whisky, bagpipes and poetry. The high point of the Scottish celebratory calendar is, of course, **Hogmanay** (New Year's Eve, 31 December). Most Scottish cities, notably Edinburgh, now host their own festivals on New Year's Eve with music, dancing and midnight fireworks, and there are less formal celebrations through-out the country.

Tipping

Tipping is not really essential in self-service cafés and bars, but is usually appreciated in restaurants (where a tip is not included in the bill, the tip should amount to around 10 per cent) and by hotel luggage porters and taxi drivers (the tip in these cases can be whatever you think is appropriate for the service you have received).

Tourism Information

Information on tourism in Scotland is available in the

GOOD READING

Banks, Iain *The Wasp Factory*, *The Crow Road*, *Complicity* and *Whit* (Little Brown). Uniquely strange stories with Scottish settings by one of Scotland's most prolific contemporary writers.

Burns, Robert (1982) *Bawdy Verse and Folk Songs*, written and collected by Robert Burns with an introduction by Magnus Magnusson (Macmillan). The entertainingly rude side of Burns's work and character.

Gauldie, Robin (2000) *Walking Edinburgh* (New Holland). Twenty-five original walks in Edinburgh, Central Scotland and Fife, by the author of the *Globetrotter Guide to Scotland*.

Gibbon, Lewis Grassic (1932–34) *A Scots Quair* (various publishers). Sweeping trilogy set in the northeast at the beginning of the 20th century.

Gray, Alistair (1981) *Lanark* (Canongate). Surreal story, Gray's magisterial magnum opus.

Kelman, James (1994) *How Late it Was, How Late* (Polygon). Uncompromising Booker prize-winning, stream of consciousness account of alcohol-soaked streetlife.

Kennedy, A L (1993 and 1995) *Looking for the Possible Dance* and *So I Am Glad* (Secker & Warburg). Quirky, intelligent, touching novels.

Prebble, John (1968) *Glencoe* (Penguin). Highly readable account of the tragic massacre.

Prebble, John (1970) *The High Girders* (Penguin). Gripping account of the Tay Bridge Disaster of 1879.

Scott, Sir Walter *Rob Roy* (various publishers and editions). Swashbuckling romanticization of the outlawed MacGregor chief, set in the late 17th century and recently filmed starring Liam Neeson in the title role.

Stevenson, Robert Louis (1886) *Kidnapped*, *Catriona*, and *The Master of Ballantrae* (various publishers and editions). Three historical romances set in Scotland during the turbulent era of the Jacobite risings.

Welsh, Irvine (1986) *Trainspotting* (Secker & Warburg). Amphetamine driven, frighteningly funny and filmed with Ewan MacGregor, Johnny Lee Miller and Robert Carlyle.

United States, Canada, South Africa, New Zealand, Australia, Germany and in many other countries from the offices of the British Tourist Authority (BTA).

Photography

Film and photographic essentials of all kinds are readily available in all Scottish towns and cities (though be warned that film usually costs more at tourism hot spots). Light for photographic pur-poses can be tricky at any time of the year, and you may need a fill-in flash on grey days. Film speeds of 100–200 are generally the most useful.

INDEX

Note: Numbers in **bold**
indicate photographs

abbeys *see* churches
Abbotsford House 50
Aberdeen 88
Aberfeldy 81
accommodation 45, 55,
   63, 76–77, 90–91,
   106–107, 121, 123, 125
Alloway 53
Anstruther 74
Arbroath **19**, **85**
Argyll 66
   Forest Park 69
   Wildlife Park 68
art 26–27, 39
Ayrshire 53

Badenoch Highlands 98
bagpipes **20**, 114
Banchory 86
Bannockburn 71
Barrie, James Matthew 84
Bass Rock **48**, **49**
Bell, Alexander Graham 37
black houses **15**
Borders 46–54, **52**
Braemar 86
Brechin 85
bridges
   Forth Railway Bridge
      17, 43
   Forth Road Bridge 43
   Kyleakin, Skye **114**
   Old Bridge of Dee,
      Aberdeen 88, **89**
   River Tay, Dunkeld **88**
   Tay Railway Bridge 82
   Tay Road Bridge 82
Brodie, Deacon William 33
Burns, Robert 23, 51, 53

Callanish **108**, 116
Callander 69
Calton Hill **39**
Carlyle, Thomas 53
Carnegie, Andrew 72
castles **46**, 70
   Balhousie Castle 80
   Balmoral Castle 86, **87**
   Blackness Castle 44
   Blair Castle **81**, **104**
   Braemar Castle 86
   Broughty Castle 84
   Caerlaverock Castle 52
   Castle Campbell **71**

castles (cont.)
   Castle Fraser 89
   Castle Girnigoe 104
   Castle Sinclair 104
   Claypotts Castle 84
   Crathes Castle 87
   Culzean Castle 53
   Dollar Castle **4**
   Drum Castle 87
   Duart Castle **112**
   Dunrobin Castle 103
   Dunnottar Castle 87
   Dunvegan Castle 114, **115**
   Edinburgh Castle **30**, 32,
      38
   Eilean Donan **28**, **99**
   Ferniehurst Castle 49
   Floors Castle 48
   Glamis Castle **84**
   Inveraray Castle **68**
   Inverness Castle **97**
   Kellie Castle 74
   Kindrochit Castle 86
   Kinloch Castle 113
   Loch Leven Castle 72
   Menstrie Castle 71
   Neidpath Castle 51
   Red Castle 85
   St Andrews Castle 75
   Stirling Castle **70**
   Tantallon Castle 48, **49**
   Urquhart Castle 96
Central Scotland 64–75
churches
   Dryburgh Abbey **50**
   Dunfermline Abbey 72
   Edinburgh High Kirk **34**
   Glasgow Cathedral 59
   Greyfriars Kirkyard,
      Edinburgh 37
   Holyrood Abbey,
      Edinburgh 36
   Inchcolm Abbey 72
   Iona **22**
   Iona Abbey **11**
   Jedburgh Abbey 49
   Kirk of St Nicholas,
      Aberdeen 88
   Melrose Abbey 50
   Queen's Cross Church,
      Glasgow 60
   Rosslyn Chapel 44
   St Andrews Cathedral **75**
   St Machar's Cathedral,
      Aberdeen 88
   St Magnus Cathdral,
      Kirkwall 118, **119**
   St John's Kirk, Perth 80
   Tron Kirk, Edinburgh 35
Civil Wars 13

clan system 22
Clava Cairns 97
climate 7, 45, 76, 90, 91,
   107, 110, 121
Crail 74
Cramond **43**
Cullerlie Stone Circle 89
Culloden Moor **14**, 97
Cupar 73
currency 19, 123
customs 122

Dalwhinnie 98
dancing **21**
distilleries *see* whisky
Dollar Glen 71
Dornoch 103
Doune 71
Drumnadrochit 96
Dumfries 51, 52
Dunbeath 103
Duncan, Admiral Adam 83
Dundee 82, **83**
Dunfermline 71
Dunkeld 81

economy 19
Edinburgh **23**, 31–44
   Calton Hill 39
   Charlotte Square **41**
   City Chambers 34
   Dean Gallery 42
   Dynamic Earth 37
   General Register House 40
   Georgian House **42**
   Gladstone's Land 33
   Grassmarket **37**
   John Knox House **35**
   Lady Stair's House 33
   Mons Meg 32
   National Gallery of
      Scotland 40
   Observatory 39
   Old College 39
   Outlook Tower 33
   Princes Street **40**
   Royal Botanic Garden 43
   Royal Mile 32–37
   Royal Scottish Academy 40
   Scotch Whisky Heritage
      Centre **33**
   Scottish National Gallery
      of Modern Art 42
   Scottish National Portrait
      Gallery 41
   West Register House 42
emergencies 125

festivals 125–126
   Edinburgh Festival **24**, 38

festivals (cont.)
   Edinburgh Tattoo **38**
   Hogmanay 38
   Up Helly Aa 11
film 28
flag 18
Fleming, Sir Alexander 40
flora and fauna **8**, **9**, 66, 97
food 29
Forfar 84
Fort Augustus 96
Fort William **10**, 94
Fortingall 8
Fraserburgh 89

Galashiels 49
Galloway 51
Gearannan 116
Glamis 84
Glasgow **16**, **56**, 57–62
   Art Gallery and Museum
      27
   Barras Market 59
   Botanic Gardens **61**
   Burrell Collection 62
   City Chambers 58
   Collins Gallery 58
   George Square 58
   Glasgow Green 58
   Glasgow School of Art
      59, **60**
   Glasgow Science Centre
      60
   Hampden Park 62
   House for an Art Lover 62
   Hunterian Art Gallery 61
   Kelvingrove Art Gallery 61
   Kelvingrove Park 61
   Kibble Palace **61**
   Lighthouse 58
   Pollok House 62
   Tall Ship 60
   Tenement House 59
   Willow Tea Room **59**
Glencoe **13**, 94
government 18–19
Gretna Green 52, **53**

Helensburgh 69
Helmsdale 103
Highlands 92–105, **92**, **103**
   Highland Clearances 15
   Highland Gatherings 15,
      21
history 10–18
holidays *see* festivals
Hopetoun House 44

Industrial Revolution 16
Inverarary 68

Inverness 97
Irvine 54
islands 6, 108–120
  Arran **66**
  Barra 117
  Benbecula 117
  Bute 67
  Canna 113
  Colonsay 111
  Eigg 113
  Gigha 111
  Hebridean Islands **113**
  Inchcolm 72
  Iona 113
  Islay 110, **111**
  Jura 111
  Lewis 115
  Muck 113
  Mull **112**
  Orkney 117
  Outer Hebrides 115
  Rhum 113
  Shetland 119
  Skye 113, **114**
  St Kilda 117
  Staffa 113
  Uists 117

Jedburgh 49
John O'Groats **105**

Kelso 48
Kingussie 98
Kinross 72
Kintale 100
Kirkcaldy 73
Kirkoswald 53
Kirkwall 118
Kirriemuir 84
Knox, John 34

language 21
Largs 54
Lerwick 119
Linlithgow 44
literature 22–24
Livingston, David 62
lobsters **19**, **29**
Lochaber 94
lochs 6
  Etive 68
  Leven **72**, **73**
  Lomond 68, **69**
  Morar 99
  Ness **96**
  Torridon **100**

Mackintosh, Charles Rennie 58–62
Mallaig 99

Mary, Queen of Scots **12**, 48, 49, 73
Mauchline 54
MacGregor, Rob Roy 69
Melrose 49
  Trimontium Exhibition 50
money see currency
monuments
  Burns Monument, Alloway 53
  Dugald Stewart Monument, Edinburgh 39
  Greyfriars Bobby, Edinburgh 37
  Melville Monument, Edinburgh 41
  National Monument, Calton Hill **39**
  National Wallace Monument, Stirling 71
  Nelson Monument, Edinburgh 40
  People's Palace, Glasgow 58
  Sir Walter Scott, Edinburgh **23**, 41
mountains, hills and peaks 6–7, **100**
  Aonach Mor 95
  Arthur's Seat 35, 37
  Ben Nevis **95**
  Cairngorm 86
  Goatfell, Arran **66**
  Grampians 79
  Mull of Kintyre 67
museums **98**
  Andrew Carnegie Birthplace Museum, Dunfermline 72
  Burns Cottage, Alloway 53, **54**
  Burns House Museum, Mauchline 54
  Clan Cameron Museum, Achnacarry 95
  Fife Folk Museum 73
  Hunterian Museum, Glasgow 61
  Huntly House Museum, Edinburgh 35
  Inverness Museum 97
  Kelvingrove Museum, Glasgow 61
  Laidhay Croft Museum 103
  Lighthouse Museum, Fraserburgh 89
  Linlithgow Heritage Trust Museum 44
  Museum of Childhood, Edinburgh 35

museums (cont.)
  Museum of Scotland, Edinburgh 36, 38
  Museum of Transport, Glasgow 61
  People's Story Museum, Edinburgh 35
  Royal Museum of Scotland, Edinburgh 38
  Scottish Maritime Museum, Irvine 54
  Scottish Museum of Football, Glasgow 62
  Shetland Museum 120
  St Andrews Preservation Trust Museum 75
  Ullapool Museum 101
  Writers' Museum, Edinburgh 33
music 24–26

Neuk of Fife 73
North Berwick 48
North Queensferry 72
North Sea oil **18**

Oban 67
Oswald, James 25

palaces
  Bishop's Palace, Kirkwall 118
  Earl Patrick's Palace, Kirkwall 118
  Earl's Palace, Kirkwall **119**
  Falkland Palace, Kirkcaldy 73
  Holyroodhouse, Edinburgh **36**
  Linlithgow **44**
  Scone Palace, Perth 81
Paolozzi, Sir Eduardo 27, 42
Park, Mungo 50
Peebles 50
people 20–29, **20**, **21**, **24**, **29**, **54**, **102**
Perth **78**, 80
Picts 10, 117
Pitlochry 81
Pittenweem 74
politics 17–18
puffins **9**

Quiraing **116**

Raeburn, Sir Henry 39
Ramsay, Allan 23
Rannoch Moor **6**
red deer **8**
Reformation 12, 34

religion 22
restaurants **25**, 45, 55, 63, 77, 91, 107, 121, 123–124
rivers **92**
  Almond **43**
  Dee **89**
  Tay **78**, 79, **83**, **88**
Romans 10

safety 7, 125
Saxons 10
Scots 10, 117
Scott, Sir Walter 23, 51
Selkirk 50, **51**
shipbuilding 61, 82
South Queensferry 43
sport 27–28, 98, 110
St Andrews **74**, 75
Steinacleit Cairn 116
Stevenson, Robert Louis 24
Stirling 70
Stonehaven 87
Stornoway 116, **117**
Strathpeffer 102
Stuart, Charles Edward 14, 99
Sumburgh **120**

tartan **20**, **21**, **102**
Tayside and Grampian 78–89
Telford, Thomas 95
Thurso 105
Tobermory 112, **113**
tourist information 122, 123
tours and tourist routes 6, 42, 49, 52, 68, 74, 80, 85, 87, 89, 103, 105, 107, 116, 124
transport 45, 55, 63, 76, 90, 106, 121, 122, 124–125
Traquair House 51
Trossachs **64**, 68

Ullapool **101**
useful contacts 45, 55, 63, 77, 91, 107, 121, 123

Vikings 11, **26**, 105

Wallace, William 12
Wars of Independence 11
Watt, James 16
Western and Northern Isles 108–120
whisky 20, 29, **33**, 86, 94, **111**
Wick 104